home

home
tales of a heritage farm

Anny Scoones

with illustrations
by Molly Lamb Bobak
and Bruno Bobak

HEDGEROW PRESS
2004

The following poems
are published by permission of their authors,
who individually retain copyright of their poems:
"At Anny's Stable," by Lorna Crozier, p. 170
"Anny's Eggs," by Susan Musgrave, p. 17
"Dear Matilda and Mabel," by P.K. Page, p. 118

Published and distributed in Canada by
Hedgerow Press, P.O. Box 2471, Sidney,
B.C. V8L 3Y3   hedgep@telus.net

National Library of Canada
Cataloguing in Publication Data
Scoones, Anny, 1957-
Home: tales of a heritage farm / with
illustrations by Molly Lamb Bobak
and Bruno Bobak
ISBN: 0-9736882-1-1
ISBN: 0-9736882-0-3 (pbk.)
1. Scoones, Anny, 1957 – Anecdotes.
2. Glamorgan Farm (North Saanich, B.C.) –
Anecdotes. 3. Farm life – British Columbia –
North Saanich – Anecdotes. 4. Historic farms –
British Columbia – North Saanich – Anecdotes.
S522.C3 S36 2004   C818/.603 22
C2004-906322-7

Text design: Frances Hunter
Cover photograph: Robbyn Gordon

Printed and bound in Canada
First printing, 2004
Second printing, 2005
Third printing, 2006
Fourth printing, 2011

*To the people, nature
and spirit of North Saanich,
and to Marilyn*

INTERIOR WITH PINK LAMP

Photograph by Robbyn Gordon

Contents

GLAMORGAN FARM *is one of the oldest farms on Vancouver Island. In 1852, Governor James Douglas and the Hudson's Bay Company acquired the Saanich Peninsula from the First Nations people for a reported one cent an acre. Six hundred acres became Glamorgan Farm, which was bought by Richard John, a farmer from Glamorganshire, Wales, in the 1860s. John arrived with his wife, Ann, and their five children. They grew oats and raised cattle on the farm. Their family home was built on the site of the present grandstand at the Sandown Raceway. A large quince bush that grew at the entrance to their farm, on what is now the Pat Bay Highway, still flourishes in the pavement alongside four lanes of traffic. Plans have recently been made to bring the quince bush home.*

The John farm stretched across what is now the Victoria airport almost all the way out to Swartz Bay, currently the BC Ferries terminal. Hired hands built the great log barns from local timber. These buildings are still in use, and they are in remarkably good condition. Because there was no sawmill on the peninsula that could cut the huge logs for the interior beams, these were shipped up from California. The barns' heavy iron door hinges were forged in Hamilton, Ontario, and brought out to the coast.

Glamorgan Farm's main barn has two distinct features: the barn is built in a cross-shaped pattern, and it is held up by its roof, in a design similar to that of a suspension bridge. The floor of the loft curves out from the centre to support the enormous weight, making it resemble a Viking ship turned upside down.

The log house where I live today was once a home for farmworkers.

It sits down a slope from the barns in a grove of indigenous Garry oak trees. In the meadow and forest across the road, behind the ramshackle barns at the Sandown Racetrack, are the original John orchard of plum, cherry, pear and apple trees, a daffodil wood and an old mill pond.

The Johns are buried at Holy Trinity Church, a small, wooden-shingled heritage church down the road at Pat Bay. When Richard died, the farm was divided among his four sons (his daughter was excluded). This was the first of many property divisions.

In the years since its founding, Glamorgan Farm has had approximately nine owners. One of these was Sam Matson, who owned the farm in the 1920s. Matson was a colourful local character and owner of The Daily Colonist *newspaper. He also built Victoria's Royal Theatre, began ferry service to the Gulf Islands and started the local bus line. Matson had a passion for raising prize Jersey cows. He lived in a stone house located just around the corner from the barns on the old farm, where the Legion Hall sits today.*

A large part of Glamorgan Farm was expropriated for the new airport during World War II. In the 1950s, the Sandown Racetrack bought a sizeable piece of the farmland along Glamorgan Road. Live harness racing still takes place there on summer weekends.

Today, Glamorgan Farm consists of just over eight acres within the Agricultural Land Reserve. I bought the farm in 2000 and am slowly restoring the old barns, log by log. In my will, I have left the farm as a public heritage park. It has always felt as if it belongs to the people, not only to me.

Morning

MY DAY BEGINS at four in the morning with a few severe leg cramps. I lie in my brass bed under my faded blue eiderdown and look out the window, watching the dawn arrive around the old log barns, their red tin roofs wet with dew. If I lie still, the cramps will usually go away, but sometimes they move to the soles of my feet.

Because of the slanted ceilings in my attic bedroom, it is difficult to hang large paintings. So, on the painted wallpaper I have hung only some small paintings and photographs: Mum when she was young, naked on a beach, building a sandcastle, and Gran shucking peas in the shade of their garden at Burnaby Lake. Next to my bed is an old watercolour Dad did of Mum with a flushed face and a blue scarf, sitting at a table.

On my dresser are ten glass dragonflies. I found them in Victoria's Chinatown for a dollar each. My favourite poster is pinned to the wall above my dresser. I found it in a trash can on a Naples street twenty-five years ago. I was sitting outdoors at a tiny café on a cobblestone lane, drinking vermouth from a filthy green glass, when I looked down and saw this poster of three little dolls with beige faces and plain expressions, dressed in white smocks, bonnets and aprons. They had delicate hands with fingers slightly curved, and they were hanging from a wall by their apron strings. The poster was advertising an opera called Lo Trattenemiento de Peccerille – Entertainment of Little Girls.

Sometimes in the middle of the night I think I hear noises. I worry that it might be a raccoon going after the chickens, or maybe an intruder. I grab the flashlight and the small hatchet from under the bed and traipse outside in my rubber boots. Sometimes I have to perform this nighttime patrol during the most ferocious of storms. I march around the barns, in and out of the dark lanes and passageways, determined to defend the farm at any cost.

As I lie in bed at this early hour, my mother will usually telephone me, or I'll call her. There is a four-hour time difference between North Saanich and Fredericton, New Brunswick, where she and Dad live. She usually starts off by saying, "Bruno just went to Super Foods with his coupons, so I can talk to you. He'll be picking over the tomatoes for hours." I'll describe the weather I see outside my window. Sometimes, when it has been stormy, I'll tell Mum how the rain and wind pounded the tin roof. We agree that March is a particularly dreary month. As Mum says, "It's as if one is sitting on a toilet and nothing happens!"

One morning Mum described a recent snowfall. The night before she had strapped on her cross-country skis and skied along the river, under the moon, among the black trees, all the way to the Princess Margaret Bridge and back.

"What if you had fallen?" I asked in alarm, and Mum said, "Then I would have died on an ice floe, like an old withered Eskimo."

Down in the kitchen, I light the fire in the wood stove, make a big pot of coffee, then feed Kitty and the dogs, Havel and Baby Alice Mary. All three like to cluster around the warm stove among the rubber boots and drying damp gloves. Havel licks Kitty's wet eyes while Baby Alice Mary stares at me, drooling for a bite of my toast. Often it is still dark outside, so I light a candle and sit at the kitchen table with a mug of coffee, to have a little think. Years ago, when I worked in England with a children's theatre company, a chubby boy in shorts, with bruised red knees, told me that he enjoyed sitting on a rock "to have a little think." I know exactly what he meant. I sit and gaze at the voluptuous scarlet amaryllis on the windowsill or the collection of old blue and white enamelware on the stove. Sometimes I'll write down my thoughts in my journal; other times I let them float away. One morning on the phone Mum said, "There's something wrong with Bruno — he sits and stares for hours in front of his face," and I thought, it must be genetic.

Sometimes I'll write to Mum, updating her on what I'm reading. Lately, I've been obsessed with Captain Wentworth from Jane Austen's *Persuasion*. How, I wonder, did Jane Austen know such deep, secret things, when she lived such a seemingly dull life? Or I'll write Mum about what I plan to grow that year. She likes to hear about the grape hyacinths and violets sprouting up in the lawn, rather than about how my septic tank is backing up because the previous owner never had it pumped.

I record the farm activities in a scrapbook. It's a large book crammed with many items: photographs of the farm before I bought it, showing piles of rubbish and rusted balls of barbed wire; ribbons from the Saanich Fair and an article I wrote the year my purple cabbages were eliminated. Even my property deed is glued into the scrapbook. There are lists of future farm plans, business cards from local beekeepers and fence-builders, and tips from oldtimers on how to deworm a horse.

Before long it is time to go outside and do the morning chores. One thing I've learned on Glamorgan Farm: there will always be something unexpected waiting for me.

The Spooky Place

BEFORE I BOUGHT GLAMORGAN FARM, I used to walk by it every morning with my dogs. We lived down the road on Ever Lasting Farm, a small place on flat land with no trees and a house that leaked. I taught horse riding at Ever Lasting Farm and kept a grand array of heritage chickens and ducks, along with a calico cat named Annabelle.

Havel would lead the way on our morning walks, his mastiff muscles rippling, his yellow Lab nose to the ground. He was always working, always observing, always anticipating what turn we might take next, what the rustling under the hedgerows of wild roses, gnarled fruit trees and spindly honeysuckles might reveal. Baby Alice Mary, a portly black Labrador, swaggered behind. She often paused, eyes half closed, taking in the faint spring scent of the pale pink blossoms from the wild plum trees on the other side of the ditches. In the spring the ditches along the road are full of watercress. The woods are full of nettles, which make wonderful soup, and the meadows provide mushrooms. Mum calls North Saanich "the Land O'Plenty."

The dogs and I had a routine for our morning walk. We'd go down Glamorgan Road to a wooded trail that we'd follow past the pungent skunk cabbages sunk in the black bog, and wade through the high brown grass of the meadow to the hidden daffodil wood. Baby Alice Mary would dip herself in the deep, dark mill pond, and then we'd stroll back towards home, behind the rundown racetrack. In rusted trailers on the property lived grooms who smelled of whiskey and had ochre-stained lips from years of smoking hand-rolled cigarettes.

As the dogs and I returned along Glamorgan Road, we always passed deserted Glamorgan Farm. Its huge barns sat stolidly on the hill. Creeping morning glory was swallowing up the log structures, which had begun to rot from a hundred years of West Coast dampness. The farm had been owned by the neighbouring racetrack since the 1950s. The owners used it to stable extra racehorses and to house some of the grooms, and also as a place to dispose of debris; rubber tires, plastic buckets, used horse needles and trash filled the well. Tall poplars lined the pot-holed driveway, which was littered with beer cans. Some of the poplars were wrapped with barbed wire to create a fence for the horses, and the barbs poking through their delicate bark had stunted their growth.

On one of her visits, Mum had dubbed Glamorgan Farm "the Spooky Place." We thought that it should be allowed to rot back to its natural state – let the rain and growth and sun and insects take the logs back to the ground from whence they came. The farm had been on the market for years, but nobody wanted to take it on. Even the "For Sale" sign had decayed, almost disappearing over time between the moss-covered remnants of a handmade stone wall.

For twelve years I walked past Glamorgan Farm every day. Then one spring morning, a morning like many others, the dogs and I headed up the road. The sun was coming up and the plum blossoms in the hedgerow were opening. There was a thin mist on the hill, but I could see the great red roofs of Glamorgan Farm. Quite suddenly, completely surprising myself, I decided to buy it. I spent an anxious day scraping together savings, divorce money and loans, running between the bank and the real estate office and the lawyer. By nightfall, I was the proud but overwhelmed owner of one of Vancouver Island's most historic farms.

The next morning, instead of going for our walk, the dogs and I went to Glamorgan Farm. The first thing I did was to cut the barbed wire from the "populars," as the high-heeled, perfectly coiffed real estate lady had called them.

The Letter

ONE OF MY BIGGEST CONCERNS about buying Glamorgan Farm was what I would tell Mum. I wanted her to be as keen and as optimistic about cleaning up the old farm as I was. Mum always told me I was just like Gran, her mother, constantly looking for things to fix up and save, constantly taking chances. I wanted to tread carefully in breaking the news. Should it be a surprise on her next visit? Should I tell her on the telephone? Should I ask my friend and lawyer, whom Mum also loves and trusts, to make the call? In the end I decided to write her a letter.

> *Dear Mum,*
>
> *Please sit down and get yourself a vermouth. I have exciting news. I bought the Spooky Place — don't panic. It's a wonderful place, and I can hardly wait to fix it up.*

I know you will be shocked, but trust me, it was a good decision. Here are some reasons why.

The log house where I'll live sits in a grove of pines. It has wood floors, a stone fireplace, a pantry and a wood stove in the kitchen. The windowsills in the living room are wide enough to sit on, and the view from these is of a gnarled Garry oak wood beyond a meadow. The staircase is narrow, leading upstairs to two little bedrooms — one for you and one for me. The ceilings are slanted, and the old glass in the windows is wavy. From my room I can see all the red roofs of the barns. The roof of the house is green. The man at the racetrack told me that they ran out of red tin, so they used green instead.

There is practically no rot in the great logs, but in a few years I may have to re-chink (with cement) them. The chinking used in the old barns was called oakum. It was a coarse substance made from horse hair, hemp and, I think, coconut twine. I am going to paint all the walls white. Your paintings will look so great on these grand, high walls. I'm going to hang your big oil, the one you did when we were at Long Beach that stormy weekend — the painting with the dramatic purple sky and the two tiny figures (us!) on the expansive silver sand. And when you come to stay, we can sit by the fire and I'll read philosophy to you, or

Auden's poetry, or Jane Austen, or a life of Peter the Great.

I just bought a book on heirloom plants. Don't worry — it was second-hand and hardly cost a thing. I am planning to plant hollyhocks and giant sunflowers against the side of each barn. It's funny — there are no flowers or fruit trees here, except for two magnificent pears. I want to put in an heirloom apple orchard. Remember the Golden Russets from England? You never see those trees any more. I ordered seven from a local nursery. I wanted the old standard size, the huge branching kind, but I could only get semi-dwarfs. That means I can call my orchard "Anny and the Seven Semi-Dwarfs."

And now I must plan the big move — how to transport all the chickens? Golden Boy, with his flaming red comb and deep amber plume, will have to ride in the front seat of the car.

Love, Anny

A Commune of Chickens

ONE OF THE LOG BARNS on Glamorgan Farm houses the Naked Neck chickens. They are a rare chicken breed, originally from Hungary, thought to have been crossed with wild turkeys. Consequently, they have no feathers on their necks.

Naked Neck hens lay large brown eggs. The rooster of the flock is Mr. Pasternak. He is handsome, with white feathers, a flowing green plume, and a very red and wrinkled neck. He has thirty wives, who every so often become fed up with his maleness and, impelled by some prehistoric Slavic impulse, take Mr. Pasternak to his knees in a frenzy of cackling, squawking, pecking and wing-flapping, leaving him cowering and tormented in a corner.

One day after one of these serious feminist altercations, Mr. Pasternak's neck was not only bleeding but dislocated. It formed a sort of S-shape. I carried him immediately to an isolated, dark pen I call the chicken clinic, where I dressed his neck with warm salt water and gently manipulated it back to its normal position.

Mr. Pasternak lay on a bed of fresh straw and was fed soft white bread for several days until he felt better. He was then fitted with a woollen dickey, tagged with Velcro for easy removal, which protected his neck not only from angry hens but also from sunburn and frostbite.

The Naked Necks share their poultry abode with other chicken residents. The Barred Rock hen is considered a heritage breed. The birds have beautiful grey and white stripes, and one could say that they are a little less emotional than the Naked Necks, not so prone to fly off the handle. The Barred Rocks do have a rather unfortunate trait, however – they all grow up to have club feet. (For this reason they prefer to have their photographs taken in deep snow.) Their disability requires that they have a weekly chicken pedicure to remove the debris that gathers between their toes during their busy daily routines. A little brush and a pan of diluted iodine do the trick. As the Naked Necks look on with disgust, the Barred Rock dipping takes place every Sunday afternoon.

There are other hens who reside with the Naked Necks and Barred Rocks. The Polish Crested is a small, delicate hen who lays white eggs. Mum says these hens look like the Queen Mother, with plumed hats that hang in long strands over their

NAKED NECK ROOSTER

Watercolour by Molly Lamb Bobak

elegant faces. The Buff Orpington is a large golden hen, originally from England. The Buff Minorca is a small, shy hen from
the Mediterranean. The Araucana is a South American hen with
multicoloured feathers who lays eggs with blue and green shells.
And, of course, no poultry pen is complete without a bantam.
The little bantam hen on Glamorgan Farm is named Belle. She is
a Silkie and looks like a white ball of fluff. Her eggs are tiny.

When I give farm tours to local children, I tell them I go on
an Easter egg hunt every day, finding coloured eggs of various
shapes and sizes hidden in nests and boxes, buried in straw or
warmly tucked under a hen's feathered breast. After I have collected the eggs, I wash them and place them in cartons for sale.

My first year on the farm, there was one other group of residents in the poultry barn on Glamorgan Farm. These were the
"meat birds." The chicks came from a breeder in Alberta, and
they were bred to grow plump within about six weeks. I thought
it would be okay; these chickens could have a free and healthy
life, pecking and scratching in the dirt and compost, until the
day came when they would have to go and "have their tonsils
out" with a nice man in Duncan.

Unlike egg-producing chickens, the meat birds all looked
identical. As chicks, they were balls of blonde fluff with soft pink
beaks and feet. I offered them clumps of grass and rich black soil
full of grubs to encourage an interest in the outdoors, but from
day one they showed no interest. It was as if the chicken intel-
ligence gene was absent. The chicks just stood around, and occasionally one would die if it forgot to drink or if another chick
stood on it for too long.

As the chickens grew larger, the situation became ridiculous. The meat birds had to be carried outdoors to get some
sunshine, and carried back inside if it rained. The legs of two of
the meat birds buckled from their bulk, and they lay helpless on
their sides. Other birds had heart attacks. It became a freak show,
watching these man-made birds, all breast and bowed pink legs,
ballooning to a repulsive weight. It was so difficult to witness
that I had their tonsils taken out two weeks early and vowed never to raise them again. I would rather eat a sinewy old rooster.

Anny's Eggs

Friday evening and it's Anny's for eggs,
her eggs all different
sizes, a few so big they won't even fit
in the carton she tries her damndest
to squeeze them into. Some are pale blue
like the moon on those nights I believe
grief comes to me on wings: who was it called
hope that feathered thing.

Sometimes the barn is empty; you'll catch Anny
leading her grey horses home from the pasture,
a few scatty chickens nattering or bickering
at her feet depending on how lucky they've been
getting lately. Last week two roosters got reduced
to soup in her stockpot: rape is one thing
she won't forgive in the barnyard.

Her black dog sighs when I arrive
and when I leave, Anny's eggs in the bursting
carton the perfect measure of sorrow, or so
I lead myself to believe.

—Susan Musgrave

Old Naked Neck Cock
and Herb Soup

Boil up an old rooster, preferably a Naked Neck.
(The French think the older and tougher the rooster,
the better – you are going for the flavour with soup,
not the texture.) Simmer for at least a day; two days
is better.

Discard the carcass. Surprisingly, an old bird
raised outdoors gives off very little fat, so there's
no need to skim the broth. Add fresh-grown herbs
(oregano, thyme, parsley, chives and dill all work
well), cooked nettle tops or garden vegetables for
a soup.

If you like to eat gristle, you can save the rooster's
feet to eat, but remember to remove the toenails and
spurs; these are quite sharp.

Variation: You can also use the Naked Neck broth
for cooking (excellent in stir fries), substituting it
for oil.

Free Pears — Yum!

I HAVE NEVER BEEN ABLE to figure out why certain years produce bumper crops — what circumstances are in place for prolific growth. One year North Saanich had an outbreak of tent caterpillars. Every apple tree was covered in squirming, fuzzy, sticky creatures that oozed green slime when you crushed them. You could hear them crunching the apple leaves at night. People told me that tent caterpillars came in droves every seven years, but seven years after that outbreak they did not return. So I'm not sure I believe in the cycle theory.

There are two pear trees on Glamorgan Farm. I love the shape of the pear tree. It is so distinctive. The tree is shaped like its fruit, bulging with growth at its base and tapering at the top into short branches that jut straight up towards the sky. The leaves are thick and stiff and shiny green, a perfect shape and texture to flutter like a flock of busy, excited birds. In the spring, the pear tree's branches are thickly covered in white blossoms with pale pink centres. The blossoms turn into hard little russet-coloured pears, and by early autumn, these are ready to eat.

The pears on Glamorgan Farm do not keep long without turning; their centres become soft, brown and pithy within days of picking. Timing is everything when harvesting fruit. There is only one day in the entire year when the fruit is at its best. The birds, particularly the crows, recognize this day, and they flock to the trees at dawn, cawing with excitement and anticipation. After this day, the fruit begins to fall, bruising itself on the parched lawn below. Bees and ants have their turn at it then.

One year the pear trees on the farm produced too many pears. Every branch bent with the weight as if the tree was weeping, and some of them snapped. The birds had their fill and so did I, bottling for many days and nights, varying my recipe with ginger, cinnamon and honey. I gave buckets and buckets of the peelings to the cows – so much that their manure began to smell like a sweet, mild disinfectant. I gave bags and bags of the pears away to my friends. I even bought a dehydrator and dried pears late into the evening. Still, it looked as if I had hardly made a dent in the trees. Their branches continued to hang heavily into the cooler nights of autumn. Every morning there was a new ripe crop on the branches and a fresh pile of pears that had fallen onto the dewy grass in the night.

One late evening as I was boiling yet another set of jars, I had an idea. I would put the pears out on the road for people going by to take away. I found a piece of plywood, slapped a coat of blue paint on it, and wrote in big white dripping letters "FREE PEARS – YUM!" I was a bit anxious as I considered what would happen if nobody took them. I might suffer from "pear rejection." It was the same feeling I'd had when I'd thought of setting up a roadside stand to sell a huge crop of zucchini and green beans. How embarrassing it would be at the end of the day to see that nothing had left the cart! (I never did go through with the vegetable stand, and much of the produce ended up on the compost.)

The next morning I filled two buckets full of pears and lugged them down the gravel driveway. I set them up beside the wooden flower tub of petunias, leaned the sign against the fence and went about my chores. People walking by the farm took one or two pears, but by nightfall the buckets were still mostly full. A sinking feeling of pear rejection began to creep in.

Early the next day, however, when the dogs and I took our stroll around the property, we had a surprise. The pears were gone, and so were the buckets.

I found more buckets, filled them with fresh pears, and put them out again. Only a few were sampled during the day by passersby. But the next morning the pears were gone again, along with their buckets, and two empty buckets were stacked neatly under the poplar tree. This routine went on for eleven days. On the twelfth day, I found a jar of pears labelled "Spiced Nutmeg Pears — Old North Saanich Recipe" sitting in the petunias. The jar was decorated with a green silk ribbon. The Pear Fairy had completed her mission.

It so happened, on a grey and drizzly afternoon that winter, when the clouds were low and the cedar boughs drooping, that I visited a nearby old folks' home to tell them about historic Glamorgan Farm. After my talk we sat in the lounge, and people told me about the old North Saanich they remembered: the trains that had come out to Pat Bay, bringing families to the seaside for picnics; the dirt lanes lined with huge cedars; the country dances in the evenings at the community hall, when the women would bring blackberry pies.

We had tea and looked at old photographs. Then we had dessert. Someone brought out a wooden tray covered with embroidered cotton napkins and white porcelain bowls. Floating in the bowls, in a delectable golden juice, were the most delicious nutmeg pears.

Mum's Pear Chutney

Mum says this chutney keeps forever. It is delicious with a Naked Neck omelette, a roast duck or pickled eggs.

Find yourself a gnarled old pear tree, unpruned for many years and laden with little pears. Pick only the underripe pears and fill a big bag with them.

Once you get home, cut the pears into small chunks. Leave the peel on, but remove the cores. Put the pear chunks into a large saucepan. Add one large onion (chopped), a handful of grated ginger, 3 cloves of garlic (peeled and chopped), the zest of one lemon or lime, ½ cup brown sugar and at least 1 handful of raisins. Sprinkle in a little allspice, powdered ginger and powdered cinnamon. Stir these ingredients together, then cover the saucepan and let it stand on the counter overnight.

The next morning, add half a cup of water and bring the ingredients to a slow boil. Let the chutney simmer for several hours, stirring occasionally and adding more water as necessary, until the mixture becomes thick.

Remove saucepan from heat, and let chutney cool. Bottle it in clean jars and seal.

NORTH SAANICH WILDFLOWERS
Watercolour by Molly Lamb Bobak

Interior with Pink Lamp

THERE IS NO BETTER TIME to clean the house, sort out drawers, spruce up the farm and complete unfinished business than before Mum comes to visit from New Brunswick. I begin the preparations days in advance, starting with her bedroom. I am determined to clean thoroughly ever since she complimented me with, "Oh, Anny, you are just like Gran, you don't care about a clean house. What a bore, to have a clean house."

Mum's bedroom is upstairs, opposite mine. Both bedrooms are small, with slanted ceilings and wooden-framed windows with brass latches. Mum's room has the brass and iron bed. I painted the iron an off-white enamel a while back, and before her visits I shine the brass knobs.

Mum and I always have a laugh about that bed and where it came from. Years ago, when I worked for a theatre company in Vancouver, the bed was used on the set of a well-known play.

When the play finished its run, I borrowed the bed, as it was set to go into storage anyway. Then I came down with scarlet fever. Mum came out and stayed with me in my apartment while I lay semi-awake under the cool sheets, only sometimes aware of the ships blowing their horns in the harbour and the smell of Mum's cigarette smoke from the other room. Mum would go for walks and pick daisies at English Bay, then come home and do paintings of them. One day, all of the theatre people came to visit me, bringing white and yellow freesias that filled the apartment with their delicate, sweet smell.

As my friends gathered around me, I suddenly remembered I was in the bed. Nobody said a thing. I still have the watercolour Mum made of the daisies and freesias, signed in pencil at the bottom, "For Scarlet Anny."

The brass and iron bed made it to Glamorgan Farm, and for Mum's visits I cover it with a handmade blue cotton quilt I brought from Fredericton when I moved away from home. Over that I put Gran's red Hudson's Bay blanket, then a duvet, because Mum says she feels the cold more now. But Mum refuses to sleep in the fresh cotton sheets. "It will save money if you don't have to wash them," she says. So she sleeps on top of the quilt instead.

Also in Mum's room is a small bookcase filled with books we have collected during her visits. These often spur the philosophical conversations we have at night. There is a biography of

Tolstoy, Auden's *Collected Poems*, a history of Britain's kings and queens, a guidebook called *Wild Flowers of Vancouver Island*, several Jane Austen novels and a collection of poems by Stevie Smith. Before Mum's visit, I dust off these books. Once, during a dusting spree, I turned to the Stevie Smith poem Mum has talked about for years as her favourite. I had never read it, but Mum had explained many times how wonderful it was, always quoting the famous words "not waving but drowning." I sat on the blue rag rug in her room reading the poem, and when I came to the lines "I was much too far out all my life / And not waving but drowning," they made me cry. Rarely a day goes by now when Stevie Smith's lines do not run through my head.

On Mum's dresser are some necessary toiletries: Ozonol, which she swears is a cure for everything, Yardley's Rose Powder, Nivea Cream and Tums. After travelling, Mum sometimes feels the need for gelatin suppositories. We go to the drugstore and always make the same malapropism: "Don't go near the grassy knoll – a bullet may come from the book suppository." We laugh like crazy and make a spectacle of ourselves in front of the people lined up to buy lottery tickets.

Mum usually visits in the spring, when shrubbery on the farm is in full bloom. I put a blue glass jug of pink honeysuckle on the table by the window, and a Mason jar of daisies on the dresser. Her window looks out on the Garry oak meadow. On the windowsill are wine bottles from her visits, now used as candle holders.

Next, I clean the glass on the paintings in Mum's room with Windex. There's a watercolour she did of Gran's pale mauve plum tree in a meadow on Galiano Island, a brown charcoal drawing by Dad of me asleep at two years, and a small oil by Mum's father of his jade collection against a yellow bowl of oranges. I always have to straighten the paintings, as they've become crooked on the walls. Perhaps the old log house is settling, or maybe it is the deep, slow rumbling of earthquakes only the walls can feel. Beside Mum's bed are some photographs. One shows her father standing in a hay field, moustachioed and looking quite distinguished in a straw hat, a scythe resting against his overalls. Mum said that he turned to farming after his nervous breakdown.

Lastly, I place on the bed "Molly's Itinerary," a carefully typed list of things to do and people to see. Most of it has to do with food. "Monday: pick nettles and make soup. Tuesday: pick rhubarb and make chutney. Pull out burdocks. Wednesday: stew up old meat bird and clean out freezer. Boil up old kidney." In addition to domestic duties, Mum and I go on outings, half-day trips and visits to local places. We always visit the oldest church in British Columbia, which sits quietly in a valley on a carpet of bluebells, moss and fallen leaves from apple and maple trees.

Mum uses two tools on the farm: a mattock, for digging out the deep tap roots of determined weeds, and a pair of long-handled clippers, for cutting back the invasions of morning glory and blackberries. For years, in her determination to stop the invasion, she would often clip my clematis vine. I finally transplanted it to a safer location.

On our walks in the wild meadows behind the racetrack, Mum picks bouquets of buttercups, daisies, berries and a fuzzy pink flower, then sits at the kitchen table and paints them. But her favourite subject is my living room. She will sketch it, and then, when she goes home to her attic studio in Fredericton, make big oils of the dark green couch and plum curtains, the soft green light that flows through the panes of wavy window-glass onto tables of books, candles and lampshades. Her most recent was titled "Interior with Pink Lamp."

In the evenings I light a fire in the grey stone fireplace. The huge pitch-covered pine cones from the back field make fine kindling. Sometimes Mum and I will take our supper in the living room, dining on nettle soup or chicken broth.

After we finish eating I read philosophy and history – or sometimes a novel – to Mum, whose sight is rapidly failing. Sometimes she can joke about it. In her recent painting of a New Brunswick hockey game, some of the burly, red-sweatered players were missing legs; their bodies ended with their shorts.

The living room has high, freshly plastered ceilings. A square cut in the ceiling leads to Mum's room – it's an old-fashioned way of heating the upstairs. Several of her oils hang on the living room walls. There is "Long Beach," which shows an ominous pale-yellow and purple sky with billowing clouds rolling in over a silver strip of sand. "Remember when we lit the beach fire and that seagull stole your bagel?" Mum always recalls. Above the piano is "San Juan Island," a deep ochre meadow with a few dark trees. We laugh when we remember the mausoleum at Roche Harbor there. Up in a scrubby, dry forest, behind a historic limestone quarry, was a grand-columned shrine erected by a wealthy local character, a certain Mr. MacMillan. In a large concrete circle stood six cement chairs. Through the lichen and mildew, the words on MacMillan's chair read, "Elk, Business Man, Husband and Christian." On his wife's was the inscription "Wife of MacMillan."

"What would Dad put on his chair?" I once asked Mum.

She replied, "Oh, he'd leave a message for me, one of his little poems: 'When you go out, I get gout.' Honestly."

Sometimes I'll play tunes on the piano and Mum will guess the songs. She says I have bad pitch, like Dad. ("Pitch burns well and keeps me warm," I say.) She guessed five out of six tunes on her last visit. The one she missed was "Aloha." She said I didn't have the right rhythm.

We go to bed early and leave our windows wide open to smell the last bit of the wood smoke from the chimney. Mum says, "*Listen* to the frogs!" as we drift off, me under my quilt and Mum on top of hers.

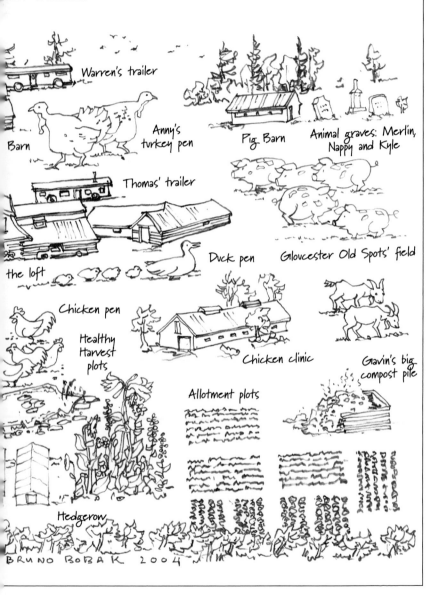

Warren's trailer

Barn

Anny's turkey pen

Pig Barn

Animal graves: Merlin, Nappy and Kyle

Thomas' trailer

the loft

Duck pen

Gloucester Old Spots' field

Chicken pen

Healthy Harvest plots

Chicken clinic

Gavin's big compost pile

Allotment plots

Hedgerow

BRUNO BOBAK 2004

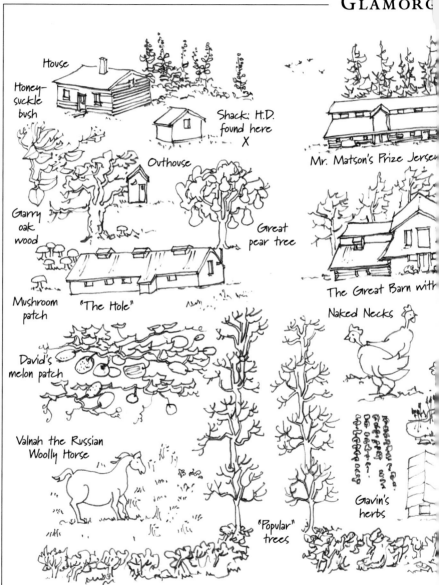

House

Honey-
suckle
bush

Shack: H.D.
found here
X

Outhouse

Garry
oak
wood

Great
pear tree

Mr. Matson's Prize Jerse

Mushroom
patch

"The Hole"

The Great Barn with

Naked Necks

David's
melon patch

Valnah the Russian
Woolly Horse

Gavin's
herbs

"Popular"
trees

Purple Turkeys

ONE OF THE MOST rewarding summer projects on Glamorgan Farm is raising turkeys for the autumn and Christmas celebrations.

The turkey chicks arrive in a small cardboard box. They may be bronze-breasted or white. Mum tells a sad story about a white turkey she had as a child in Burnaby Lake. It was very lonely and used to sit up in a tree, watching her below talking to her donkey.

Last year I picked up my little box of ten baby turkeys and kept them in my bedroom for a few weeks, until they were strong enough to go into their pen of fresh hay in the barn. The babies lived in a large container under a red heat lamp beside my bed. My bedroom became incredibly warm. After a few days it smelled of heated grain and warm feathers, a rather homey, comforting smell. It was as if bread was baking, or a stew was simmering in the old farmhouse.

The baby turkeys stretched their sinewy pink necks above their box with curiosity whenever I undressed, flossed my teeth or filed my corns – they really took an interest in my life. I was flattered. As they grew, they began to do a sort of fly/hop over the edge of their box, and I would find them nestled in my good shoes or sound asleep in a lambswool scarf I bought for Mum in Scotland. I began to find turkey droppings in my jewellery box, on my leather-bound copy of *War and Peace,* in my pantyhose drawers and on my pillow.

I became quite attached to the turkeys. We all loved to listen to Danny Finkleman on CBC on Saturday night, and I gave them toast every morning. Whenever I folded laundry, they all gathered around, as if I was going to make a great speech.

When the turkeys began to roost at night on my bedposts and lamps, I knew the time had come to move my friends to their own room in the barn. Their quarters had a ramp and a special door that opened into a courtyard of grass.

One by one, I carried the turkey babies out to their new dwelling. But I noticed a curious thing. Now that the turkeys were bigger and more mature, it was easy to see an unusual disfigurement of their beaks. They all had a slight overbite, and they found it very difficult to eat their new diet of grains and corn. The man who builds my fences said, "Those turkeys have cleft palates!"

This was not going to be profitable or practical, I thought

at first. Then I discovered that the turkeys loved blackberries. There was a large blackberry bush in the corner of their pen, and one morning I saw them gathered around the bush doing little hops to reach the fruit. I picked a handful and threw them down, and the turkeys went wild, pecking at the berries as the juice ran down their wrinkled necks onto their white-feathered breasts.

After that, every day at noon, I'd take a bucket and pick berries from all along the hedgerows on Glamorgan Road. I'd arrive back at the farm with my legs torn from the thorns and my hands purple from berry stains, but the turkeys were grateful, and they always ran to the gate in anticipation. A local bakery gave me free day-old bread, which was also easy for the turkeys to chew.

And so it went, every day through August and on into the cool fall. When we were ready to harvest the squash and pumpkins on the farm, the nice man who takes out the chickens' tonsils arrived and loaded the birds into the back of his pickup. He returned them the following day in plastic bags ready for the freezer.

What a surprise I had.

The man chuckled as he lifted the bags from the back of his pickup truck. "Well, your birds were sure easy to see," he said as he handed me ten forty-pound purple turkeys.

"Oh, God," I murmured. "It was all that white bread and those blackberries."

In the days to come, various friends came by the farm to pick up their Thanksgiving turkeys. Later, most of them admitted that they hadn't been able to fit the birds into their pans or ovens and had had to saw them in half. But we all agreed that the purple turkeys with the cleft palates were the most succulent and tender we had ever eaten.

Blue Moons

THE FRONT MEADOW of Glamorgan Farm is gardened by a group of six mentally and physically challenged adults. With the help of a horticultural therapist they formed a co-operative and called themselves the Healthy Harvest.

The Healthy Harvest gardeners come to the farm all year round, trudging up Glamorgan Road in yellow rain-gear and heavy backpacks even on our wettest, chilliest winter days. They have a small greenhouse and a hut that sits on the side of the road and serves as a vegetable stand in the summer. A double row of neat raised beds leads to one of Glamorgan Farm's log barns, where the gardeners store their tools and supplies. Shelves are jammed with organic fertilizers, old gardening magazines and flowerpots. They also have a composting toilet, hand soap and a kettle.

Beside this log barn is the horse pasture, which houses an old Appaloosa named Duke and a young, strong Russian Bashkir

Curly horse named Valnah. Valnah's ancestors came from Siberia. Instead of horse hair, these unusual heritage horses have wool that grows in waves and curls. When Valnah sheds his coat every spring, the nesting birds rush down to collect it. It's not every bird that can line its nest with Hungarian chicken feathers and genuine Russian wool. The Healthy Harvest gardeners gather up Duke and Valnah's droppings and dig them into their organic garden beds.

Not long ago, the gardeners took over another field on the farm. They plan to create a public park for people to visit, rest, stroll and snack in. It will have a lily pond, a herb garden, fruit trees, blueberry bushes, edible flowers and heirloom vegetables, all grown in a rich mixture of fallen Garry oak leaves, manure and wool shed by the Russian horse.

David is one of the most dedicated gardeners. He can often be seen late into the night, sometimes in the pelting rain, other times under the moon, sifting soil for his special French pumpkins or constructing a shelter out of Popsicle sticks, twist-ties and plastic bags for his tropical melons. He once explained to me that a gardener must have the patience of a stone and the skill of a brain surgeon. "Unlike you, Anny," he added, "who are best as a keen observer."

One summer David grew melons and squash in a corner of the orchard. Their reaching tentacles became intertwined, and many of the melons and squashes cross-bred. Heirloom melons bred with pumpkins. Cantaloupes crossed with zucchinis. Cucumbers cozied up with honeydews. The blue Hubbard squashes held hands all summer with the pale yellow Moonbeam melons. We called the offspring "Blue Moons." They were smooth and round, a pretty grey-blue shade.

Visitors to the farm were enchanted with these new vegetable-fruits, and David regularly explained their genesis to interested passersby. One day as I was collecting the eggs, I overheard his conversation with a group of older walkers, tourists from England in Tilley hats and sensible shoes.

"What conditions do these extraordinary fruits prefer?" one man asked David.

David answered, "What I know about these fruits is that they do best in the years that wearing long pants makes you feel uncomfortable."

The Englishman wrote down the advice as his wife nodded her head with intense interest. They were anxious to get back to England and inform their local nursery about the new Canadian propagation.

One day a group of cyclists stopped by the farm. In their skinny black racing suits, alien goggles and helmets with fins, they resembled a swarm of busy wasps. They parked their cycles by the fence and approached David in his melon patch, asking for water to refill their bottles. But David persuaded them to sit for a minute and sample his melons.

Once he had a captive audience, David launched into his health spiel. "People concerned with health and nutrition, such as yourselves, will be interested to know that the nectar you are consuming has been carefully cultivated from three organic heirloom fruits in a replica of tropical conditions. You are consuming the vitamins from three separate species in one fruit."

David sold nine melons to the cyclists, earning enough money for the Healthy Harvest to buy a new hose and sprinkler. The cyclists are regular visitors now at Glamorgan Farm.

The best day of sales that summer came towards the end of August, in a week so hot that you could smell the pine cones lying in the dry yellow grass and see the giant sunflowers lining the Healthy Harvest garden path bow their heads with thirst. Across the road and down the hill, a music festival was underway. Rows of turquoise porta-potties had been brought in, and local food vendors set up a village of shacks with pretty awnings and black cauldrons. There were booths selling organic soaps, assorted teas, crystal balls and colourful woven cloth from Latin America. Thousands of people lay on blankets under the blazing sun, listening to live music being played on the tented stage. At the end of the first evening, after the headliner had yelled a final "Thank you," people wrapped in shawls and Peruvian sweaters crawled into tents in a far section of the field. The neighbourhood became silent under the stars.

The Healthy Harvest gardeners had built a vegetable cart

from one of the sulkies we found in the bush on the farm. They'd painted it bright yellow with some leftover paint, replaced the wheels, and varnished the dry shafts. The cart was hauled to the roadside every morning, loaded with produce to sell. They relied on the honour system, putting out a tin can for money amidst lush bunches of greens, bouquets of purple cosmos, and heaps of squashes and melons in shades of ochre and orange. That evening, because one of the hens was having kidney trouble, I forgot to bring in the sulky. The next morning, it was gone!

The dogs and I walked up the road, thinking that somebody might have wheeled the sulky into the blackberry brambles for a lark. But there was no sign of it. Down on the racetrack field, campers were beginning to fire up their camp stoves. A local band was warming up, and spectators were starting to arrive. I felt terrible for the Healthy Harvest gardeners, who had worked so hard on their cart.

The heat rose gradually as I went about my chores. I had to dig a burial plot for the hen, who had died in the night. I chose a spot alongside the plots I'd created for an old pony, a spastic turkey with a gimpy leg and other farm animals that had died under my care. They all had very nice graves marked with smooth grey boulders.

While I was performing this sad chore, Baby Alice Mary waddled down to the racetrack, hoping to discover a treat at the source of the wonderful aroma drifting up our road. I set off to get her before she disappeared into the crowd.

At the main gate, I asked a man in an orange vest, "Did a rather portly black Labrador waddle by here in the last hour?"

"Yes," said the man. "I saw her heading towards the performers' tent." Before I could reach the performers' tent I was stopped again. "I am only here to find my dog," I pleaded. From there, I could see Alice Mary following a musician with a hot dog. "May I please go in and get her?"

The man let me through. I passed a band being interviewed by a local radio host and a guy with a fiddle warming up. The performers' tent was packed with musicians tuning up and drinking cans of Coke. And there in the middle were David and the sulky cart. People were snapping up the Blue Moon melons, and festival volunteers were cutting up fruit for the performers. One weathered-looking fellow threw the rind sideways before charging onstage to roars of applause. I grabbed Alice Mary and left.

The last night of the festival was a warm, clear evening, and I decided to sit out on the deck. The last band hit their final notes at midnight. I imagined all the tents and camp stoves being packed up into Volkswagen vans. I took a stroll around the farm to check on things before bed, and down by the gardens I saw the sulky cart, parked back beside the fence.

David had sold everything. The tin can was full of coins. The gate leading to the gardens was wide open, because David has trouble handling the clasp. A few months earlier he had left the gate to the horse pasture open after he'd trudged up into the bush to empty the composting toilet. At two in the morning, a policeman knocked on my door and said, "Are you missing a couple of horses?" He told me that they were down the road at the bottle depot.

David would be back the next morning to cultivate his melons with mushroom manure and make more plastic tents for the younger melons. He had already started the plants in plastic domed cups, the kind you get when you order a Frappuccino at a trendy coffee bar. David collects the cups in a burlap sack, going right up to customers sipping on their crushed ice, caramel and coffee concoction. "The cups are to propagate my melons," he tells them. "Would you like to place an order for the spring?"

Little Anny Rooney

IT IS SO FUNNY that I've ended up living across from a racetrack.

Although I was born in North Vancouver, I grew up in Fredericton. Mum and Dad are both artists, and both of them had taken jobs as artists-in-residence at the University of New Brunswick. I was five at the time, and my brother, Sasha, was fifteen. The first house we lived in there, a small wooden one painted dark yellow with white trim, was on Grey Street. The university stood on the hill nearby.

Grey Street was lined with elm trees, and our house was a block from the ambling brown Saint John River, which every so often could be seen carrying large piles of yellow foam slowly along its banks. Mum always said, "It's that damn McCain chip factory upriver in Hartland, but I love the man because he gives to charity."

Fredericton was okay as a place to grow up, but I always felt my heart was in the West. In New Brunswick there was skiing on white gleaming hills in bright sunshine under a blue sky, but I preferred to be on the beach, collecting shells and paddling on splintery logs with my Gran, who lived on Galiano Island. I spent most of my summers with her while my parents were off painting in Spain. At the end of August, Mum would come to pick me up.

There are three smells I still recall from my time on Galiano as a child: the burning bark as it mixed with the damp sea air, the sweet peas Gran always had on her blue tablecloth, and the creosoted logs of the wharf at low tide.

My main companions on Galiano (apart from the neighbour's free-running red hen and Gracie, a wild cat I'd tamed) were my thirty-two trolls, each of whom had a suitcase. They made the trip with me every summer. One day, as usual, we were all on the beach. Mum was with us, along with my brother's girl-friend, Kate. It was a sloping sandstone beach, and there were little pools with blue mussels and white sea anemones, tiny lim-pets and darting bits of sea life – the tidal pools had lives of their own. Mum and Kate, a buxom young woman who usually wore skimpy crocheted tops and miniskirts, were sunning themselves on the warm sandstone.

The trolls were sunning themselves as well, around a little pool. Some wore rubber bathing caps – party balloons I had cut in half. My favourite troll, Isabelle, was paddling on a log. Her best friend, Enid, a troll who could never get wet because she was so furry, was on shore preparing a picnic.

A dramatic event then took place. A ferry went past, causing several large waves to roll towards shore. One of them came up over the pool, and my companions were swept away in one wavy second (along with their turquoise Tonka jeep, which only Isabelle knew how to drive). I screamed as the trolls were washed out to sea. Mum came tearing down the rocks, followed by big, sexy Kate, who was naked and had a cigarette in her mouth. Kate bounced over the rocks at Mum's command, both of them slipping on the slimy green seaweed. All the trolls were rescued. They had floated into the sewer-pipe outlet – the area where I swam because it was always so warm – and had found shelter amongst the secretive purple starfish and dark, mysterious stones.

When I was six, my dad produced a series of artworks called "Studies of Anny Sulking." They culminate in a large oil painting of me sitting in an overstuffed chair and looking absolutely disgusted. I have on a school uniform, and my fist is jammed into my chubby cheek, pulling it sideways in an angry mood. The great gobs of paint are red, grey and ochre. I was mad, probably at having to go back to Fredericton. Mum says I held onto Gran's smock for mercy as Mum tried to get me to pack my bag to leave at the end of one summer.

Dad decorated our house on Grey Street. He hung gold

ANNY SULKING

Charcoal drawing by Bruno Bobak

cherubs from the ceiling in the dining room, which had walls covered in red felt. In one room he covered the walls with gold and silver Peter Jackson cigarette wrappings. I remember him sitting there one night with a brandy, having a heated debate with a viola player from the university. The viola player said something derogatory about Canada, and Dad became very agitated. He leaned over the table and said, right into the viola player's face, "That's the charm of Canada, for Christ's sake – nothing happens! We are peaceful, kind, gentle and wise. It's our role in the world." I was passing through the room with my bowl of Shreddies (my usual dinner, which I ate with the trolls), and his words had a profound impact on me. I think Dad is fiercely loyal to Canada because he came here as a three-year-old emigrant from Poland and lived under a bridge with his brothers Ernie and Henry and his stepmother. (His father came too, but he was off looking for a job.) They ate cabbages and restaurant scraps.

On hot summer days, Mum and Dad would often go out sketching on a country riverbank. I'd join them, packing up the trolls for a day's picnic and raft trip among the reeds and rushes. One afternoon the summer I was eleven, I left the trolls to sunbathe in the grass while I walked down a dirt lane. Soon I came upon a dry meadow. A sway-backed old palomino hung her head over a rusted fence. She smelled like an ungroomed, hot, perspiring horse – there really is no smell like it. I knew about horses, so I was not timid, and I scratched her fly-bitten face. A man drove by on a tractor. He told me her name was Missy. Then he said, "You want her? You can have her."

When we got home that night, I begged Mum and Dad to let me take Missy. They had a huge fight about it; Mum said it was fine, but Dad didn't agree. I cried and threw a tantrum through-out the night – even the trolls didn't get one bit of attention. Finally Dad capitulated, and the next day Mum and I drove out to the farm and paid the man a hundred dollars. The farmer said he could keep Missy for us for a while, but we needed to find a place for her closer to our house in town. I asked at the Pony Club where I took riding lessons, but because Missy was a mixed breed with short legs and a big stomach, they wouldn't board her. They suggested Wilmot Downs, the Fredericton race-track.

I rode my bike to the track as soon as I could. Wilmot Downs was in the Fredericton Exhibition Grounds, a huge paved area surrounded by a chain-link fence. At one end of the track were rows of rundown barns where the racehorses lived. Some of the grooms lived there too. I bounced over a muddy road full of potholes until I saw a red-faced man with no teeth sitting in a chair next to a steaming manure pile. He was drinking a can of beer. A racehorse in a black harness walked by, pulling a tired-looking jockey on a cart.

"Do you know if I could board my horse here?" I asked the man with the beer.

"Yeah," he answered tiredly. He waved his hand towards a dark stall with garbage all around it and a tin roof folded back from a recent storm. The man told me his name was Shine.

I spent a weekend scrubbing the dilapidated stall, painting the door dark blue with some spare paint one of the grooms gave me, replacing the burned-out light bulb and hanging the sign I'd made on the door: "Missy – Owned by Anny Bobak." I hung my equipment on some rusted hooks in an orderly line.

That summer I practically lived at the track. I rode Missy in the infield and helped the grooms bathe their racehorses. I tidied, raked and organized my area, then helped the grooms unload bags of oats. They called me "little Anny Rooney." By two in the afternoon, most of them were passed out drunk in their stalls.

I wanted to be like them, part of the racetrack life. "Hey, Anny Rooney," they'd call in the late afternoons when they stumbled out of their stalls into the bright sunlight. "Put that old nag of yours six feet under!" I'd just laugh and make some cheeky retort.

At sundown the track would go quiet. The pencil-legged, bandaged, over-trained bay racehorses, smelling of liniment, would go to sleep in their straw beds. Sometimes I slept with Missy in the hay for the night. Shine had a hot plate in his stall, so I could make toast or heat up cans of Chef Boyardee macaroni and cheese, which I bought at a local convenience store. One night when I went in, Shine was snoring off a bottle of whiskey.

In a sleepy stupor, he pulled me down into the hay and planted a big toothless kiss on my mouth.

"Shine!" I said. "Wake up!"

Everything was okay after that, except that Shine was embarrassed and I felt sorry for him. "Son of a bitch, Anny Rooney," he said. "I didn't know it was you. I must have been dreaming." That toothless kiss may be the reason I have never touched whiskey.

The following summer, I got a paying job at Wilmot Downs. My job was to collect the winning racehorse's urine in a tin cup after every race. There were usually about ten races, held on Sunday nights. The grandstand would be packed with people screaming and cheering and waving their race forms in the air. The air smelled of beer and cigarettes and the greasy chips being fried at the stand.

Great overhead lights lit the gravel track where the horses pounded in a group across the finish line, their jockeys leaning forward over them, dressed in coloured silks, muddy goggles and white pants. The winning horse, nostrils flaring and ribs glistening, would prance its way to a small grassy area just past the finish line. My job was to place the tin cup, which was attached to a long stick, under the horse – if it was a male, that is; around the back if it was a female – then whistle, which was supposed to make the horse relax and urinate. I took the full cup to a man in a wooden booth for drug testing. By nine o'clock the man was so drunk that he usually spilled most of the urine on the counter. I was paid one dollar a race.

With my ten dollars in my jeans at midnight, I'd sit in the hay with Missy as the crowds ambled out the gates and across the paved parking area. About one in the morning, when I knew that all was dark and quiet, I got on my bike and rode home to Grey Street, along the streets of small wooden houses, past the dilapidated Willet Fruit Company and the Chestnut Canoe Factory, through a baseball park and down a shrubby trail. I parked my bike in the garage beside my parents' green Buick, went into the silent house, got a bowl of Shreddies and took it to my unmade bed. The trolls, by the end of that summer, sat neglected in a row on my shelf.

There was a wonderful smell in the barns on those late race nights — a combination of hot urine and spearmint liniment mixed with the heated gravel from the track, wet leather and pine-tar hoof paint. On summer Saturday nights on Glamorgan Farm, thirty-six years later and five thousand miles away from Wilmot Downs, the same smell floats up from the barns and the faded yellow grandstand at Sandown. I love it as much as I ever did.

The Hole

WHEN I BOUGHT Glamorgan Farm, the description of the property read, "Eleven Structures," although I saw only ten. I didn't have much time to ponder the mystery. I began the clean-up of the farm immediately, removing truckloads of rubbish from inside each building and from the fields. But although the clean-up started right away, it lasted over two years. And I always avoided the building I called the "hole."

The hole had been built on a hill – dug into a hill, actually, so that when you opened the door, the floor was ten feet below. In the old days, buildings were often built in this way to contain the ground's warmth, and hay was stored in the loft for extra insulation. This barn, however, had been used as a dumping ground by the racetrack since 1952, and the trash was so deep that it came up to the level of the door. I could barely face it. I would have called a junk man to clear the whole thing out, but I was tempted by the idea that I might find a treasure in that mound – a farm relic, an antique or some other rare and interesting item. So one afternoon I screwed up my courage and began the sorting myself. I put on a pair of gloves and told myself not to look at the big picture, just to concentrate on the moment at hand. I stood on top of the heap and threw items onto the driveway. My plan was to sort the recyclable items into piles.

After several muggy hours of this, I was filthy, hot and fed up. I had pulled up over sixty rubber tires, masses of paint cans, ripped vinyl chairs with bent chrome legs (probably from the bar at the racetrack), broken fluorescent lights, dozens of toilet seats, hundreds of whiskey bottles, stacks of newspaper, assorted hardened paintbrushes and cracked plastic buckets – and no treasure was to be found. I had barely made a dent in the pile, and the driveway was a mess.

I was ready to give up. But after a bath and a good sleep, I went back the next morning with fresh resolve. Maybe a treasure lay just beyond my reach. I continued my task, uncovering cans of dried hoof ointment, orange shag carpet with cigarette burns, greasy rags, rusted pots and pans, heaps of split sewer-piping, coils of old weatherstripping, parts of oily tractor engines, a deep fryer with three inches of dusty fat still stuck to its baskets and round amber ashtrays still full of butts. There were buckets of pink lavatory soap, frayed ropes, toilet plungers and broken mirrors – but still no treasure.

I didn't completely throw in the towel, but my attacks on the trash in the hole became few and far between. One summer evening, however, as I was relaxing on the cool moss under the pear tree, a man appeared and asked in a gentle manner if I had any shop space to rent out. He explained that he and his friend were shipwrights – they repaired and built wooden boats. I showed him the hole, and we struck a deal. He and his partner could have the space for two months rent-free if he cleaned the hole out. They rented a huge metal dumpster, and in two days they had the hole emptied.

Once the clean-up was complete – no treasure was ever found, alas – the "boat boys" enlarged the windows in the building to let in more light and built a set of stairs down to the cement floor below. They covered the floor with wide ship's planking, installed a small wood stove and constructed a beautiful loft, a mezzanine, out of yellow pine that they oiled to a soft glow. Their hand tools, which had been handed down to them by their grandfathers, had bone handles fitted with brass screws. Chisels and planes were organized on a wall rack in order of tool size. The shipwrights built wall cabinets and tool chests from red cedar. Finally they hung a lovely oval carved sign outside, above their new door.

The boat boys were open for business, and they soon began to make wooden boats in many styles: flat-bottomed dories, West Coast fishing boats, and the wide but elegant "pea pod," a rowboat shaped like its namesake. They painted their vessels with thick, shiny enamels of amber and deep blues, then hoisted them high above their workbenches using brass-and-rope pulleys.

An antique set of navigation lights sat on the windowsill, one red and one blue. They had come off a local boat, an old wooden classic, as had the bent and tarnished brass propeller hung above the opposite window. There were a few black-and-white photographs of vessels the boys had restored, replacing planks and masts, then sanding and varnishing. One of these boats was the *Uchuck III,* which in her time ran up and down the coast delivering goods to the villages. I often joined the boys on their coffee breaks, and we'd sit outside in the rockery discussing the names people give their modern fibreglass boats, such as *Nauti Gal, FantaSea* or *Spicy Lady.*

The boys asked permission to build an outhouse behind their shop in a grove of pine trees – the long-needled kind whose sap-filled cones make such useful kindling. I thought an outhouse was a good idea. One evening, in a blackberry patch on the corner of the property, I noticed a piece of red metal – the type of red tin that had been used on the farm's roofs. I peered in more closely and saw a weathered, shingle-sided hut lying on its side. Two thoughts hit me at once. This would make a perfect outhouse, and this was the farm's eleventh building – a rotted little hut among the thorns.

The boat boys hauled the hut out with their truck, put it on skids and dragged it up to their shop. We threw the filthy toilet away, hosed the shack out and brushed off the cobwebs. The boys dug a deep hole and built a cedar door. I hung a blue ceramic crescent moon on it, and the outhouse was ready to be christened.

But there were other creatures eyeing the outhouse. A busy barn swallow thought it would make a lovely home, and she began constructing a nest of chicken feathers, hay and horse hair in a corner of the ceiling. Once the babies hatched, their droppings and dry bits of the nest fell onto the toilet seat. When the birds were ready to fly away, we cut a square window in the door.

Those young birds departed but the barn swallow parents return every year, diligently rebuilding their cozy nest for their new family. A group of bees – very gentle bees – built a hive on the back of the building, burrowing into a well-rotted shingle. Two canary-coloured butterflies eventually made a home for themselves behind the crescent moon. An anthill appeared in the sandy soil at the entrance, and countless spiders spun their webs across the wide, dark hole. Giant black slugs slimed their way to a private place on the underside of the toilet seat. Every day I peeled them off and fed them to the chickens.

One day while the boat boys were out delivering a "pea pod," an efficient-looking woman walked down the driveway. She wore glasses and carried a clipboard. She introduced herself as a district bylaw enforcer. She'd heard that there was a boat-building operation on the farm, she announced, and that was against the bylaw that said farms were meant to be used strictly for agricultural uses.

Thinking quickly, I told her that the boys only built boats on the side; mainly they were my farm help, making fences, feed troughs and structures for the animals.

"That's interesting," the woman said. "So what's this sign that says 'Boat Building'?" I glanced up at the beautifully carved sign swaying in the breeze.

Over the coming weeks, the bylaw enforcer was relentless in her determination to rid the farm of the boat boys. They finally had to pack up their tools, load their wooden boats onto trailers, and move to another shop. They left behind the glass-panelled doors that separated the shop from their office, and a few pulleys still hang from the pine mezzanine railing. Behind the transformed "hole," the outhouse is still home to any creature that discovers it. I go into it every so often and give it a sweep.

Not long ago, a woman called to ask if I had a barn space for rent for a weaving studio. Surely *that* would be legal, weaving wool. I could even acquire some sheep or cashmere goats to shear. With any luck, the hole may soon be buzzing with activity again.

Pickled Eggs

I ONCE ATE A TASTY pickled egg at a village pub in England, and after I'd moved to Glamorgan Farm, I decided to make pickled eggs right here. To myself I boasted that my pickled eggs would be especially wonderful, since I intended to use the fresh eggs laid by my heritage hens, in all their different shapes and sizes and varieties.

I telephoned Dad and got my Polish grandmother's recipe for pickling brine, a potent mixture of vinegar, dill, mustard and spices. I sterilized some Mason jars in boiling water. I hard-boiled the eggs and pierced them with a toothpick before placing them in the brine to be pickled. The jars filled with brine and eggs sat on my kitchen shelf, in among Mum's apple jellies, some bottled salmon, and wooden boxes of dried herbs. After three weeks, the pickling was complete. The eggs were delicious. I ate them by the fire on a cool spring evening.

That autumn, I decided to enter a jar of pickled eggs in the Saanich Fair. I repeated the pickling procedure carefully. The theme of the fair was "the olden days," so I found an antique jar with a glass lid. Mum had done a funny watercolour of my Naked Neck rooster, so I used that on the label. Part of the fair's expectation is that entrants educate the public, so I wrote a note about the heritage hens who had laid the eggs I used.

The eggs sat patiently in their jar until the big day arrived. The night before the fair, people take their displays and entries to the various tents. Everyone vies for the best space and the best light for display. It can be quite competitive. Women with huge colourful dahlias shove each other out of the way, and it is downright volatile in the home-baking section.

I carried my pickled eggs to the correct display area and set the jar down carefully. There were rows of relishes, burgundy-coloured preserves, pink herbal vinegars, and interesting-looking bottles of pickled beets and mushrooms, all tied with silk ribbons, raffia, or elegant twine. The honey in the corner, in shining shades of ambers and ochres, was labelled with exotic names like "Goldenrod and Sweet Pea," "Fireweed" and "Saanich Wildflower."

There was only one other jar of pickled eggs, but it gave me a sinking feeling — it looked so perfect. The brine was crystal clear, and three gleaming white eggs sat in perfect balance, with two sharply cut slivers of red pepper arranged against the side

of the jar. My misshapen Naked Neck eggs were plopped into a brown, cloudy brine, absent of any decoration. But taste was part of the judging, and surely I would make up ground there. I trusted Dad's recipe. His mother had pickled everything – that was how food was preserved in Eastern European countries. If you can get your hands on a traditional Slavic pickling recipe, you can't go wrong. That was why I was going to win the pickled-egg competition.

I had also made a label describing the three breeds of hens that my eggs came from: "The little egg was laid by the miniature Silkie, a small hen with extremely fluffy feathers resembling goose down. The largest egg came from the rare Hungarian

Naked Neck, originally thought to be a cross with a wild turkey, thus having no feathers on its neck. The middle-sized egg was laid by the South American Araucana hen, the shell of whose eggs is always blue or green." I had an interesting label propped up behind my jar, three unique eggs and a delicious traditional brine. How could I lose?

Judging is done on the first morning of the fair. The judges award ribbons, and sometimes they write short comments on the entries. That afternoon everything is on display for the public to see. Entrants are asked not to remove their displays until the fair closes three days later.

I love the Saanich fair and all its activity. One year Mum was here visiting, and we went to the fair on the morning of the last day. It was raining, and we watched the pig-obedience class from soaking green bleachers with the rain pouring off our hoods. Three teenagers were trying to control their naughty pigs in the mud. One pig was terribly interested in another pig and paid no attention whatsoever to his exasperated owner. But the judge, a nice blonde woman in a poncho with a clipboard under her arm, gave each of the handlers a wet blue ribbon. She explained to the spectators (Mum and me) that even though one boy had had trouble controlling his pig, his knowledge of swine ailments was far beyond what was expected from an exhibitor.

After watching the pigs, I had a caramel apple. They look so good standing in a line under the glass counter, but they are always disappointing and extremely awkward to eat on their sticks. Mum and I stood under the eaves of the draft-horse barn, out of the rain. I took one bite and then my apple fell into the wet gravel and rolled away down the hill.

Mum and I had just decided to go home and sit by the fire when we heard a great commotion coming from around the corner of the barn. A miniature horse pulling a two-wheeled cart, in which sat a huge woman in a billowing dress of light-blue chiffon, came streaking around the corner, almost running us down. The woman was screaming, "Whoa, you son of a bitch! Goddamn you! Whoa!" She had both her handbrakes on, and the wheels left deep troughs in the gravel. The disobedient horse galloped past us towards the outdoor café, where, thankfully, nobody was sitting. The cart caught the corner of an umbrella and pulled over the whole table. The top of the umbrella caught the awning above, ripping it from the building. Deck chairs went flying in all directions. The frightened horse raced on, dragging the broken cart, bits of harness, a chair, and the umbrella and ripped awning behind him. The driver tried to scramble off the cart, but her dress had become tangled in one of the wheels. Finally, she tumbled off and rolled onto the soggy grass, her dress torn off at the thigh. Her horse charged away towards the rides and the cotton-candy booths. A man in overalls ran to help the woman. She was terribly humiliated but otherwise okay. I heard her say, "That little bastard! This is the last time he'll come to the Saanich Fair."

But this year my pickled eggs were being judged. That afternoon I walked nonchalantly past the beautiful shelves of winning preserves covered in red, blue and purple rosettes. As I got closer, I could see that the blue ribbon was on the jar with the clean brine, not mine. Not only that, I hadn't even received second place! To make matters worse, I found that the judges had scrawled something on my entry tag: "Not sealed properly and leaks."

There was no way I was going to let my pickled eggs sit there for two more days with that mean note attached. But how could I get them past the old men guarding the door? Maybe I should say that I was going out of town and would not be there to pick up my eggs in two days. Maybe I should carry them out brazenly, as if I was unaware of the three-day rule. I thought of slipping the entry tag into my hand and not picking up my eggs at all – ever. At least if the tag was gone, thousands of people would not see me accused of trying to give the pickled-egg judges botulism.

I became tense as I witnessed the lines of people strolling past the shelves and reading each tag. "Do these people not have a life?" I thought nastily. "Are they so bored that they have to read every single tag?" I was getting desperate.

Finally, I couldn't bear it another minute. I marched up to the shelf, picked up my improperly sealed jar of eggs and my label and walked, as if I meant business, across the room towards the door. I could see the real world outside – the shiny tilt-a-whirl chairs spinning with screaming children, the candy-apple stand, the clown in the dunk tank, all under a big, warm, blue sky.

The old men stood up from their chrome chairs and took their positions by the door. My heart sank. "Nothing leaves this room until Monday," the stooped man in a diamond-patterned cardigan said. His friend in suspenders stood behind him. I could see people eating hot dogs out on the lawn, and a man weighing the giant pumpkins on a flatbed truck.

"I have permission," I lied. "A lady at the desk said it was okay because I'll be out of town on Monday."

"Would that have been Hilda or Joan?" the suspendered man asked the other.

"Best I go up and check," said the one in the diamond cardigan. He shuffled off towards the stairs as his friend continued to stand by the door.

"I'll wait out there in the sun," I said. Then I walked out and headed straight for the parking lot, running as soon as I rounded the corner. With brine splashing onto my shirt, I ran through the dairy barn. Black cows with clean pink udders and mouths full of green alfalfa turned their heads slowly in vague curiosity. I took a shortcut through the home-crafts building, scooted through the restored antique farm-equipment display and ran out the gate towards the field where my car was parked. I had escaped!

When I arrived home I changed my shirt and sat out on the deck. I felt like eating a pickled egg, but the judges had given me serious doubts. Because the jar wasn't sealed, was I in danger of being poisoned?

I sat and looked at the jar on the round glass table. It would be a waste of three good eggs not to eat them. I sat for a long time. Then I did a few chores. That way, if I died, at least the animals would be fed and clean for the night.

The eggs were delicious. I ate all three and waited. Nothing happened.

Pickled Eggs

Hard-boil a dozen eggs. Let them cool, then remove the shells. Set aside.

Boil together 1 quart vinegar, 1 tsp. dry mustard, 1 tsp. salt and 1 tsp. pepper. Let this brine cool, then pour it into a clean jar. Pierce each egg several times with a toothpick. Add eggs to the brine. Cover and let sit for at least ten days.

Duck Luck

THE FEMALE DUCKS on Glamorgan Farm are Mrs. Brown
and Lillian. The two of them are dear friends. Lillian is a small
white Moscovy duck with a pinkish-red bill and orange webbed
feet. Mrs. Brown, who is much older, is a stout brown French
Rouen duck. Terribly pigeon-toed, she tumbles over into the
grass if rushed. Flustered and dishevelled, she will then rise with
a clumsy action and waddle away, quacking in disgust. Lillian is
far more of a lady. Elegant, wise and subdued, she peeps rather
than quacks and waits politely for her several servings of bread
a day.

A few years back, Lillian and her husband, Alfie, were getting on in years – both of them were over five years old. In their
younger days, they would produce two families a year of at least
ten yellow ducklings, some with dabs of black on their heads.
That year, however, only two baby ducks were produced. It was

time for Alfie to "retire" so that Mrs. Brown and Lillian could spend their remaining years in peace.

After Alfie left, the two female ducks threw a pool party. They swam and dove all day in their little pond tucked in the tall, lush clover, pausing from time to time to flap and beat their wings in a manic cleaning ritual. In the coming days, their appetites increased. They grew strong new feathers and a soft undergrowth of down.

I decided that I'd keep Lillian and Mrs. Brown as pets, so I purchased ten Moscovy ducklings from another local farm. The peeping fluffy yellow babies with their soft pink bills arrived in a cardboard box. I had prepared a firewood box for them in the living room, lining it with fresh hay and placing a shallow casserole dish of water at one end. I filled a dish with Duck Starter, a high-protein feed, and hung a heat lamp from a chair for warmth. The babies were happy there. They loved hearing me practise the piano every evening, seeming to particularly enjoy "A Stranger in Paradise" and "When the Saints Come Marching In."

One night, very late, I woke to a piercing cry coming from the living room, clearly a call of distress. I climbed out of bed, over Baby Alice Mary, Havel and Kitty, and hurried downstairs. I fumbled around in the dark room and finally found the light, and there was one baby duck sitting on the footstool, peeping at the top of his lungs. The little escape artist was the duckling with the biggest smudge on his head. I put him back in the fire-wood box and returned to bed.

A few days later, it was time to move the babies to a stall in the barn between the chicken clinic and the Naked Neck nurs-ery. The move was a big event. Each duckling was individually placed in a deep basket and carried up to the barn. Little ducks are amazingly soft. They feel like mounds of jelly or furry sea cucumbers. By now, the ducklings had progressed to a deeper pan of water – something they could swim in. They seemed very happy in their new space.

The little ducks paddled in their pan while I cut open a bale of sweet-smelling hay. The hens love fresh hay fluffed up in their nesting boxes, and they were clucking in anticipation. The sun was shining, and all of us were feeling contented. As the hay bale unfolded itself into neat, square flakes, two dried and flat-tened mice, caught in an embrace, tails still intact, fell to the cement floor. I raked the chicken yard, changed the water and sprinkled some stale bread crumbs, then went about the rest of my farm chores.

Before supper I checked on the baby ducks. The day's happi-ness was shattered when I saw a pitiful sight. One little duck was lying on his back, very still, in a corner, his wet fluff stuck to his bluish-pink skin. It was the duckling with the big black smudge. I rushed to his chilled body, breathed on him and rubbed his lit-tle Buddha stomach to increase his circulation. Barely alive, he went limp and fell onto his side when I tried to stand him up. For an hour I held him under the heat lamp, attempting to do duck CPR every few minutes. I guessed what had happened – he had been in the deep pan and had had difficulty climbing out, probably struggling for a long time until he became exhausted. How could I have been so stupid, giving the babies a pool too deep to climb out of easily? My mood turned to a cold, anxious guilt.

There was no time to waste in bringing the little duck back to life. After my CPR attempts, I made a deep hay bed and tucked him in, piling up the hay around him to keep him from toppling sideways. Then I lowered the heat lamp over him. His brothers and sisters sat in a tight group, watching from the corner. I went to the house and retrieved the shallow casserole dish, filled it with fresh water, and set it down for the rest of the baby ducks, removing the deep pan. I went to collect the chickens' eggs, and an hour later, when I returned, the duckling was warm. He stumbled back to the group, his down dry and fluffy again.

After two weeks in the new stall, the ducklings were ready to join Lillian and Mrs. Brown outdoors in the grassy, enclosed pen. All of the outdoor pens are covered in fishnet to protect the birds from predators such as ravens, eagles and hawks. I had done that after the horrifying experience of seeing an eagle land on top of Golden Boy, the most handsome of roosters. One minute Golden Boy was innocently pecking and scratching in the manure pile. Then, in one graceful swoop, an eagle flew down into the pen, grabbed Golden Boy in its great talons and carried the screaming rooster away. The two of them quickly receded into a black speck against the sky. Since then I have never left the birds so vulnerable.

Curious, cautious and excited, the ducklings stayed in a tight cluster as they explored their new residence. Lillian was intrigued. She tried to herd the little group, urging them to follow her through the pen, where there was much to see – two pools, a running hose to bathe under, a lean-to for shade, a dish of corn, an unmowed section of tall clover in which to gather one's thoughts, and a shed for nesting and nighttime sleeping. Mrs. Brown ignored the new residents and continued on with her solitary pursuits. Most of the time, she sits under a shady bush, letting her days pass calmly. She is the nun of the duck world. Barren and shy, she has never laid an egg nor shown any interest in that sort of thing.

As dusk fell, it was time to herd the ducklings into their shed for the night, so that they were protected from nocturnal predators such as raccoons. Suddenly I noticed that one duckling was covered in blood. It was the black smudge duck again. Looking him over closely, I discovered a deep wound under one wing. It looked serious; stitches might be needed.

I placed the injured duckling in the chicken clinic for the night. The clinic had been cleaned after Mr. Pasternak's stay and bedded with clean straw. First thing in the morning I put the little duck in a cat crate, and we visited the local veterinarian. He diagnosed the injury as a tear from the duck's wing being caught in something, perhaps a fence.

A number of options were offered as treatment. I opted for antibiotics and hourly cleansing and was presented with a bill that totalled more than all the ducklings had cost together. I left the office with creams, pills, syringes, bottles, a bag of iodine solution and instructions to return with the duckling in three days for a progress check.

The little duck sat in the passenger seat on our drive home. He soiled the material, and to this day the deep yellow-green stain remains. I have to explain the story of the injured duck to anyone who sits there.

The smudge duck recovered quickly, but he developed a stunted wing. He also developed a dislike for water, refusing not only to bathe but even to wash his head, and consequently he always had a filthy face and a blackened, crusty bill. In the end, his funny wing and clumsy, awkward gestures spared him a trip to the dinner table (the fate of his brothers and sisters). Instead, he became Lillian and Mrs. Brown's new friend. I discovered that the smudge duck was actually a female when she laid a beautiful white egg one summer morning. I named her May, for the month she'd come to Glamorgan Farm. She was a duck born to waddle to a different drum.

The Owl

THE FIRST SIGN THAT YOU have rats on your farm is the sighting of droppings and the smell of urine – in this case, in the chicken coop. Soon after, you see the rats scurrying across the floor, and then they start to feel quite at home, waiting around in plain sight for an egg to be laid before pilfering it and sucking out the yolk. They become so tame that, at feeding time, they sit beside you while you're mixing the grain. They beg like dogs on their hind legs, waiting in the hopes that a few morsels of corn will fall on the cement floor. One of my neighbours tells me the rats at her place come out and watch television with her!

One year there was a serious and gruesome rat problem on Glamorgan Farm. In the poultry barn I had set up a chicken nursery, a small pen with a deep bed of straw and a heat lamp for twenty baby chicks. There were ten tiny Naked Necks – balls of fluff with pink, wrinkled necks – and ten "top hatters," as the Polish Cresteds are sometimes called.

When I went out to the nursery to feed the babies, I got quite a start. The rats had gnawed a hole through the floor and tried to drag a chick through. The little feathered body was wedged in the hole, its pink feet in the air, but the worst was yet to be seen. I gently pulled the bird out of the opening only to find that its head had been chewed off. I dug a small grave for the chick in the rockery beside my house.

Rats breed and grow rapidly. I have read horror stories of them chewing through house wiring, carrying fatal diseases or completely destroying an underground plumbing system. Once you've spotted them, pest control must be undertaken. But *how* is the great question. There seem to be three alternatives, according to Dave, who works for a local exterminating company.

Dave wears an exterminator's uniform – black pants and a white shirt with *Dave* embroidered on it in red silky letters. Around his waist is a leather belt weighed down with all sorts of exterminator tools – flashlights, gas mask, calculator, cell phone, spray cans, digging tools, a notebook, mousetraps, cans of bait, ropes, flares, keys, bigger flares, a small saw, elbow-length rubber gloves, hand cleaner, spongy knee pads with elastic straps and a small black plastic box labelled "Dave's Emergency Kit."

Dave first told me that he could set out boxes of rat poison. I rejected that idea after hearing about the agonizing death rats undergo when they ingest these lethal pink pellets. Apparently the poison burns the animal's guts from the inside out. The second alternative was even more horrible. A platform covered in a thick, brown glue-like substance is set out. The rats' feet stick to the board, and once that happens, you're supposed to submerge the platform in water and drown the pathetic, screaming creatures. I chose the third option: traps.

I had used a rat trap once before, in my kitchen. A rat had taken up residence under my sink, scratching and feasting every night on the compost and empty cans of dog food. When it began to chew on the wooden cupboard door, I decided that I had had enough. I bought a trap at the hardware store and set it carefully under the sink.

After dinner the dogs and I were sitting by the fire when we heard the rustling of cans falling over and then a loud snap. But that was not the end of the rat. The snap was followed by crashes, bangs, anguished screeches and shuffling sounds. I sat there in a terrible state, knowing that the poor creature was suffering. I was beside myself with guilt, and I finally went to the woodshed to get the hatchet I use to split kindling. I intended to chop off the rat's head quickly and put it out of its misery. When I returned, however, the kitchen was silent. I hesitantly opened the cupboard door, and before me lay the sprung trap. On it were a spot of blood and, under the snapped wire, a long, grey tail.

This time around, I hoped the rats would go into the traps

head first. Late in the afternoon, Dave and I set the traps with peanut butter and put them in strategic places where no other animal could be caught in them. Then I went about my chores. Before I had even cut open a new bale of hay for the chicken nests, there were four loud, crisp snaps. So the traps were a great success – on the first day.

Rats are very intelligent, and they have excellent social and communication skills. One article I read said that they will quickly learn of danger and alert each other. I could just see the Glamorgan Farm rats convening in the dirt tunnels under the henhouse floor to hear the updates: "Now, all rats be warned, do not go near the traps, no matter how tempting, no matter what the bait. We hear that marshmallows will soon be used. Do not be fooled, fellow rats!"

And so, not another rat was ever trapped on Glamorgan Farm.

All was not lost, however, as I discovered one wet dawn when I approached the chicken barn to begin the morning chores. The night rain was dripping off the barn roof. The sky was a light grey, with a promising strip of golden light behind the dark wooded hills. Sometimes on those damp mornings I can smell the sea mixed with the wood of the trees. The thistles, burdocks and morning glory seemed to have grown three feet overnight. I must clip them back, I thought. Then I got a start, and my heart skipped a beat as I glanced towards the chicken run.

Tangled in the fishnet was a large brown owl. My immediate response was sympathy. The owl looked so vulnerable, and it stared right at me with enormous yellow moon eyes, terrified and perfectly still, as if apologetic. I ran and got some scissors, leather gloves and a blanket.

I covered the owl with the blanket, leaving exposed only the sections of its wing tangled in the nylon. I cut the net from its feathers. As I did so, the owl curled its talons and grasped my hand. Surprisingly, its grasp was gentle, and it didn't struggle. When the mission was finished, I carried the owl to an open field, and it flew away.

Upon my return to the chicken pen, I found four dead rats. The gentle owl had obviously killed them and was attempting to carry them away, perhaps to its family in some rotted tree in the woods or an abandoned barn. I hoped it would be back.

Say It with Seaweed

SOMETIMES I GIVE brief tours of Glamorgan Farm to people who are interested in heritage sites. The farm is really like a small village. The dark red log barns, with their white-trimmed crooked windows, are of various sizes and shapes. Narrow gravel lanes wind in between the structures, and occasionally one sees a faded climbing rose bush struggling to hold onto an earwig-eaten log. There are a few grassy patches here and there, and freshly painted white post-and-rail fences divide pastures and meadows and gardens, animal pens and paddocks.

When I show the farm to people, I point out the broken window high in the double loft of one of the oldest barns. "At dusk," I tell them, "an owl family appears in the window. One year they had a white-faced baby." I point out the Naked Neck chickens and the Russian woolly horse and the heirloom vegetables that the Healthy Harvest gardeners grow. I show them the cross-shaped, cedar-beamed loft in the big barn – the barn where I held barn dances and community fundraisers on summer nights.

When I first moved to Glamorgan Farm, two trailers sat amongst the brambles behind one of the big log barns. The trailers housed two tenants, Thomas and Warren. They shared a homemade septic tank: an old car buried deep in the damp clay soil. There were actually seven tenants who lived on the farm. They were all very private and kept to themselves. Whenever I gave a farm tour, I was careful to avoid the trailers and cabins tucked away behind barns and in the bush. The day I bought Glamorgan Farm, I went around to each tenant and introduced myself. I talked to them about my obsession with neatness and cleanliness, trying hard not to hurt their feelings. They have all moved on now, but I remember them with fondness.

Thomas, a Polish painter from Winnipeg, lived in the trailer closest to my house, so I got to know him first, and I hired him to do odd jobs. He told me one day, as he cooked a steak on a barbecue he'd made from old bricks, that he wished he had become a monk. He had considered it once, but he met a girl instead. Every so often Thomas left a bowl of borscht on my step. He would have made an excellent monk.

All day he sat and read, or boiled soup or painted cement garden ornaments. He had painted a whale mural across the front of his trailer. One of Thomas's jobs on the farm was to catch rats. I gave him a beer for every rat he trapped.

Thomas had a few flower boxes, and one spring I gave him some nasturtium seeds, which he planted and then completely ignored. The wonderful, lush nasturtiums crept all over his deck and trailer, blooming in succulent red and orange. His last project before he moved on was a rock garden, decorated with a little Buddha and a cement snail he painted blue.

Sometimes Thomas and I sat on his plywood verandah at dusk and talked. He wore slippers, the kind that look as if they are made from a carpet. One time we were a little sad because a barn cat had died – her name was Anastasia. She was Annabelle's sister, a beautiful calico. Thomas buried her up on the hill.

"When I die, I want some of my ashes to be thrown into Pat Bay and some to be thrown here on the farm," I said to Thomas.

"I don't care where I go," he replied.

I told him that I would scatter his ashes on the farm with the rest of us. Then we sat for a moment and didn't say much. "Did you catch any rats today?" I asked finally.

"No, I think I'll try the peanut butter again. They don't really like white bread."

Thomas always kept his area neat. But another of the tenants, Warren, needed encouragement to observe the neatness code. Warren's trailer was at the back of the property, behind the barn that housed 20,000 chickens in the days when Sam Matson owned the farm.

Warren was a mechanic. He picked up temporary jobs here and there, working just enough to pay his bills before retreating to his trailer for long periods of seclusion. He was also a pack rat. When I bought the farm, his trailer was surrounded by a forest of blackberry brambles, thistles and junk: shredded orange tarps, lawn mowers, gas barbecues, motorboat engines, plastic lawn furniture, hubcaps and tires, rusted dirt bikes with no motors and a deflated rubber dinghy.

One evening not long after I moved onto the farm, I made my way through plywood scraps, plastic pails and burdocks to knock on the flimsy aluminum door of Warren's green and white trailer. I was a little concerned because I hadn't seen him for days. His truck was there, and I was worried he might be unwell. I wasn't sure about the protocol, since we're all so private. But I felt I needed to check on him, so I summoned up my courage.

It was pitch-black outside, and the frogs were singing. I could see a faint light coming from one end of Warren's trailer, so I decided to peek in the window first, just a glance to prepare me for the worst. My heart was pounding as I stepped cautiously through the tall, wet grass. But inside, there was Warren, hunched over on his bed, dipping a paintbrush into jars of paint. He was painting tiny figures and wooden houses, which he then placed on a shelf above his head, along with dozens of little people, cars, train engines and plastic tractors. I was relieved as I made my way back around to the door. I knocked softly. Warren came to the door still holding the paintbrush. The trailer was freezing, and his television was on. The place was littered with cat-food tins, ashtrays full of butts and beer bottles.

"Hi," I said. "Just checking in." I stepped inside. There was a poster on the wall of a woman with curly hair dressed in black leather and a red scarf, straddling a huge motorcycle. "That's my mother," Warren growled proudly as he stroked his moustache. "She was a real motorcycle babe." I knew it was true, because they looked so much alike.

On one shelf I saw three swag lamps, some brass candlesticks and a Russian fur hat. "Is that a real Russian hat?" I asked. "With flaps?"

"Yeah," he mumbled. "I got it at a swap meet for two dollars." I had a Russian fur hat too, I told him. I had paid twenty dollars for it in Minsk.

Once we had made that discovery, Warren reached for one of his painted cars. "I'm trying to get off the beer, so I started a new hobby," he explained. "Check this out. It's a 1940s job." There was a pause as I admired it. "I thought I would make a replica of the neighbourhood," Warren continued. "I'll have a train going through it, and this farm will be the central point. You don't have any red metal from the roofs lying around, do you?" From a closet with a broken door handle, Warren pulled out several wooden models. Each was a replica of a different barn on Glamorgan Farm. They were made carefully and with great attention to detail. He had even included the climbing rose bush on the cross-shaped barn and the black forged hinges on the barn door. The windows in the replicas were filled with the traditional wavy glass.

As I was leaving, Warren asked me if I would like to go to a swap meet with him the following morning. "Early, so we can get the deals," he said. So the next day, at the crack of dawn, we headed out for a grubby suburb of Victoria. We stopped at the Payless gas station for coffee, then drove through a maze of strip malls and stucco buildings until we arrived at a bingo hall. "BI_GO EV_RY SUNDA_," the sign read, "WITH AL_YO_ CAN EAT BUF_ET."

Men in plaid shirts were gathered in groups, smoking, in the parking lot. Inside, a grey-haired woman in a pink apron charged us a dollar each to enter. There were rows and rows of plywood tables piled high with rusty tools, crocheted pot holders, used books, plastic toys, pictures of sunsets and roses, lamps, electronic gadgets and Disney videos. I bought a jar of pickled beans from a woman who took my money without even glancing up from the *National Enquirer* she was reading.

Warren went through a bin filled to the top with model train and track parts, miniature farm animals, and plastic shrubs and trees. He pulled out a black engine with a light that really worked. After some dickering, the man selling it agreed to let it go for twelve dollars, with a plastic tractor and two little people thrown in. At another booth, Warren bargained for two fishing flies. He bought them, proudly showing them to me in his palm. Warren said the fuzzy hooks would catch salmon and that they were called "The Woolly Bugger" and "The Royal Coachman."

Next, Warren stopped at a table covered with lacquered wooden plaques. Each one had a colourful abstract design. A large sign above them read, "Say It with Seaweed." Warren and the woman who had made the plaques embarked on a long conversation about how she goes to the beach to select different types of seaweed, arranges it on the wood, and embellishes it with bits of rope and shells to bring out the texture. Warren bought a plaque featuring a sunburst of red seaweed outlined in orange, a few white shells in one corner, and a painted fishboat in the distance.

When we got home, I put my pickled beans in the kitchen and then went about my chores. Later that afternoon, as I was sitting outside on my porch, Warren walked down from his trailer carrying a yellowed cardboard box and wearing his Russian hat.

"I know you like beans," he said as he approached from under the pear tree. "These are my grandpa's old beans. Do you think they'll grow?" Inside the box were all sorts of beans – heirloom variety, no doubt.

I took the beans into the house and returned wearing my Russian fur hat from Minsk. "Let's lower the flaps," I suggested, which we did. We sat there on my lawn chairs in our fur hats, and soon it began to rain.

The Disappearance

IN THE EARLY 1950s, when the Sandown Racetrack bought all the land along Glamorgan Road, they tore down Richard John's original three-storey home and built the cumbersome concrete grandstand that still sits there today, its yellow paint peeling. From Glamorgan Farm I can look down over the meadow and see the plumes of dust rising from the horses as they jog around the track for their early-morning workouts, pulling their carts behind them. In each cart is a groom lazily dangling one leg off the back, loosely holding the cracked leather reins.

The grooms hose down the perspiring horses and moist harnesses after the workout. After the stretched tendons in the horses' thin legs are rubbed down with liniment, and their legs wrapped with woollen pads and red cotton bandages, the animals are put out for the day in makeshift paddocks. The barns at Sandown are falling down. Most have been gnawed to splinters by neurotic horses who race too often and are not given enough freedom from their dim stalls. Unmowed grassy lanes, littered with plastic pails and rubber hoses, separate the barns from one another. Sludgy pools of horse urine, leaching from the massive manure piles, collect in the ditches and potholes. The grooms at Sandown are an affable bunch, just like my old friends at Wilmot Downs. Their mildewed trailers are wedged deep in the alder woods behind the track. We exchange waves every morning as I walk by with the dogs.

When the winter rains stop, and things dry up, the horses start to train in earnest for the summer races. The grooms fix up the stalls by hanging flower baskets from the barn corners and repainting some of the trim. As the weather gets nice, they gather outside their trailers on plastic lawn chairs, cooking steaks on their barbecues.

Once racing season starts, weekend evenings are filled with the smells of French fries and dry, hot gravel drifting up the road. Every half-hour, in that controlled twang, you can hear, "They're off," followed by the thunder of pounding hoofs and people cheering on their favourites. I often wonder who is collecting the horses' urine in a tin cup. The next morning, damp racing programs and paper cups cover the racetrack field.

Baby Alice Mary makes two trips a day down the hill to visit the track. Mum calls Alice Mary a "fat, spoiled rich girl" because I bought her from a breeder. Mum says she hasn't suffered like the other dogs, whom I adopted from the pound in Victoria.

And yet Alice Mary is attracted to the not-so-sophisticated side of life. The grooms give her treats, and she can mooch for left-over French fries in the grass the day after a race. She swaggers from one trailer to the next, licking barbecues and looking for-lorn. Her routine has made her more portly than ever; she gets her annual vaccine while sitting on the floor because the vet can't lift her onto the steel table.

Alice Mary usually comes right home after she makes her rounds. I can hear her flop into her basket on the porch, heav-ing herself into a comfortable position with a gluttonous, satis-fied sigh. But one evening she didn't show up. I put the horses out in the back paddock, locked in the chickens and ducks, add-ed the manure from the big field to the compost pile, gave the goats a handful of alfalfa and got ready to settle onto the couch for a session with my *Encyclopedia of Country Living*. (I was look-ing for instructions on how to make soap, an idea I abandoned after finding them – the procedure sounds as if it would require the patience and skill of a surgeon and also make one heck of a mess in your kitchen.) But Baby Alice Mary still had not come home. I have learned that things usually work themselves out in time in country life, but I always worry when a routine changes without an explanation. Grabbing a flashlight, I enlisted Havel to come with me down to the racetrack.

The place was dead quiet and completely unlit. Havel and I walked up and down the grassy corridors between the barns, passing steaming piles of manure. There was no sign of Baby Alice Mary. I have to admit that Alice Mary has never been my favourite dog. She's a happy dog, but not very deep. She isn't sensitive and aware like Havel, who knows that his job is to protect the farm. But I suddenly realized I would really miss her if she were to leave us.

Havel and I made our way through the alder wood towards the mill pond, a place alive with the sound of the evening frog chorus. We saw a faint light through the trees, from a television, it looked like. As we got closer, we could see that the light was coming from a trailer, the kind Mum describes as a "silver bullet." I decided to ask the groom if he had seen Baby Alice Mary.

I climbed two bent aluminum steps to the sound of voices from the television. The door was open, and in the whitish light I peered in. A large groom wearing only undershorts was asleep in a black vinyl chair. His mouth was open, and there were several empty beer cans beside his bony feet. Then I saw Baby Alice Mary, also flat out, snoring on the rust-coloured couch. There were a few empty dishes beneath her on the linoleum floor. I quietly backed down the steps, wishing I could sleep that deeply.

Havel and I walked slowly back up the hill, greatly relieved. I had a deep hot bath, then got into bed under the expensive duvet I'd bought in Sidney at a chic kitchen and bath shop. I thought of Alice on the polyester couch and the man in the vinyl chair, and I thought about what my Polish grandmother used to say: "People are people." And sleep is sleep, wherever you find it.

Old Friends

I DON'T USUALLY DISCUSS the horses on Glamorgan Farm because there isn't a lot to say: horses stand in the field and graze, watching the world go by; they come into their stalls at night for their dinner; they go on gentle rides around the neighbourhood; they are groomed, bathed and clipped, and their hoofs tended to. Horses are not that intelligent or affectionate, and they can be quite dangerous, although they conjure up such romantic fantasies for people — galloping bareback on a beach (in slow motion, of course) or riding blissfully into a sunset. The only time I tried galloping on a beach, the horse fell over a log and I tumbled off, scraping my face on a large rock covered in barnacles. And as for the sunset ride, well, let's just say that it is unwise to ride in the dark, even in North Saanich. Horses spook and bolt at things — a plastic bag lying in a ditch, a car horn, a man hammering together his new deck, dogs barking, children playing ball, bicycle bells, sprinklers, branches blowing in the wind, low-flying aircraft, sheep bleating and generally everything else one might pass on a country lane.

A horse knows when its handler is tired, weak or nervous, and it takes instant advantage, often trampling or dragging the helpless handler through the mud. It knows when you are trying to catch it to go for a ride and often refuses to be caught, tearing around the field testing your patience and endurance, sometimes spraining a ligament in the process and costing you a fortune in vet bills. Horses get chills, infections and digestive disorders. For every gentle ride you go on, you spend much more time and energy grooming your filthy horse. And if a horse wants something on the other side of the fence, it will simply smash down anything in its way – including people – to get to the object of its desire.

For some misguided reason, I once operated a riding school. I had fifty little riders, mostly girls, and one summer we decided to put on a horse show for the parents and the local community. We came up with the idea of doing a "charge" – all the riders would wear red T-shirts and charge up the field into the riding ring to the music of the "William Tell Overture." They would line up in the ring, we hoped to much applause, and the audience members would then let go of the helium balloons each had been given on their way in. (This was before the days of environmental awareness.)

Of course, things didn't come off quite as planned. As a group of ten riders charged into the ring, most of the audience let their balloons go shooting up into the air. This spooked the horses, and eight riders fell off their mounts in a sudden and violent stampede. (Mum, who was visiting, was making sketches for a painting she planned to do of our "opening ceremonies." She caught this moment of chaos and reproduced it as a big oil painting, which now hangs in my living room.) Everyone was okay, except for getting mouthfuls of grit and fresh wood chips, and the horse show proceeded smoothly until we performed the "Horses in Art" display. I'd dreamed this up. Each child would dress as a character from a famous horse painting and pose just as that character did while I held up a big wooden picture frame. There was "Napoleon Crossing the Alps" and "Alexander the Great." Naturally, the horses spooked again, and the riders screamed in panic as they scrambled to hang on to their squirmy mounts. The horses ruined all the fun at our first horse show.

So this is why I rarely feel inspired to write about horses. They seem to me like boats – a money drain, an expensive hobby, and sometimes quite a hazard. But occasionally a horse with character, charm, spunk and even a sense of humour ends up at Glamorgan Farm, softening my jaded, curmudgeonly heart. This is a story about two of them.

Napoleon – everyone called him Nappy – was a pony who had lived on Glamorgan Road for years and years. The dairy

farmer down the road remembered Nappy throwing off his young daughter into a pile of brambles thirty years earlier. At one time Nappy had been the main horse in our local riding school. Misbehaving at each fair by tossing off his rider, nipping spectators or bolting as he passed by the sheep barn, Nappy never failed to win events such as "the costume class," for which we once dressed him up as a beach bum. Looking back, I think this was a humiliation for Nappy, but he did win some blue ribbons for our club. In the horse stables at the fair, spectators would smile as they petted Nappy's soft nose, because he could barely see over his stall door. Mum always said that he looked like a little moose.

Now, old and grizzled, with grey hairs all around his deep eye sockets and muzzle, Nappy had retired. But he was lonely. Every time he heard a racehorse whinnying in one of the rickety barns across the road, he ran to the fence and strained to see who it might be. I acquired a donkey named Alastair, thinking he and Nappy would be great pals, but mean Alastair simply bullied Nappy and, worse, kicked Mum and knocked her down into the buttercups. That was it – I promptly gave Alastair away to a ranch on Saltspring Island. The last time I saw him he was being led in a local parade by two strapping women and wearing a T-shirt that said, "Ride at Saltspring Trail Rides." So Nappy remained alone.

Then one scorching summer day I had a call from a woman who had bought a farm on the other side of Victoria. She wanted to grow grapes and start a vineyard. There was a decrepit horse on the property that she wanted to get rid of, and someone had given her my name. If I wanted this horse, she said, she would have him trailered over that day. Her neighbours called the horse Kyle, she told me. He had been a champion racehorse in his youth and was then put out to pasture and ignored.

I said, "Okay, bring him over." Maybe Kyle would be a nice riding horse, who knew? And I didn't want to think of him going to the slaughterhouse.

That evening, just at the time the horizon is lined with a golden trim of lace and chiffon, like a cheap prom dress from a consignment store, a rusty truck pulling an equally rusty horse-trailer came up the driveway. I paid the driver thirty dollars for transporting Kyle, and he lowered the trailer ramp at the back of the truck. We could hear Kyle inside, stomping to get out.

Nappy was at the gate, straining to see the new visitor. Kyle slowly backed off the trailer, slipping on the ramp's worn rubber mat. What a sight he was! He was extremely tall and very thin. His ribs and hip bones could be seen under his mangy coat. He had a massive rash and flaky skin covered with red, oozing sores. His hoofs were dry and cracked, and his tail was caked with manure.

The first thing I did was lead Kyle around to stretch his legs, but he limped, and that's when I noticed that his left back leg was swollen and dripping with pus. I offered him an apple. He took it, but it fell clumsily out of his mouth. Kyle had no teeth, only brown, rotting nubs.

There is really only one cause for tooth nubs in a horse – chewing on wood. Many horses, especially racehorses, are kept most of the time in dark stalls and brought out only to train and to run. The boredom that these high-strung thoroughbreds experience drives them to the point of insanity. Some develop the habit of weaving – the equivalent in humans is rocking. Some spend the hours chewing their stalls to bits, which wears their teeth down. Kyle's nubs were the worst case I had ever seen. No wonder he was so thin. What was I going to feed him?

I decided to put Kyle in the back paddock adjoining the main field for the night. That way he and Nappy could make friends over the fence, or not. He hobbled to the paddock dragging his infected leg. The first thing he did when he got there was to roll in the dirt. Next he took a drink, and then he just stood under a large cedar, his head drooping. Nappy was straining his little grizzled moose nose over the top bar of the fence. But tired Kyle could barely look up.

The next morning I woke up early. I had had a restless night, worrying that the trailer trip had been too much for Kyle and that he had died in the night or become disoriented and ill.

As soon as there was enough light to see, I put on my boots and toque (I have to wear a toque even in the summer dawn, because I get earaches, just like Gran used to), and went out to check on Kyle. There he was, his long thin neck and bony face hanging over the top fence rail, very still, right beside Nappy's furry grey head. Both had one back leg resting in the air, and both of them were sound asleep. I left the two old horses alone and went back to the house until it was time to feed them breakfast.

When the sun had risen, I went out to do my chores and tend to Nappy and Kyle. They were still hanging over the fence together, but now they were awake. I led them into the barn one at a time. After I'd fed Nappy, I mixed up a bran mash for Kyle. I thought he'd be able to slurp that down, and he did, getting it all over his face. I usually cut up apples and carrots for the horses as well, but Kyle's had to be grated. I grated my fingers, too, and I thought to myself, as my raw knuckles bled, "Anny, this is the last time you make fun of people who are romantic about their horses."

Kyle put on a little weight as the summer passed. He and Nappy spent every moment together, most days just drifting in and out of sleep under the shady Garry oak trees until their next meal was prepared. Sometimes they stood head to tail so they could swat the flies from each other's faces, although Nappy's tail barely reached Kyle's chest. When they scratched each other, Kyle had to stoop, his long sinewy legs spread like a giraffe's.

If Nappy walked around a corner out of sight, Kyle would break into an anxious sweat and call frantically until he saw his pony friend. One hot afternoon Nappy unlatched the gate and wandered around the maple tree, out of Kyle's line of sight. I was watering the cabbage patch behind the house when I heard an almighty crash – the sound of boards snapping, and then a ruckus of grunts and groans and thrashing. One of the Healthy Harvest gardeners came running around the house and yelled, "Kyle's lying on the driveway! He broke the fence!"

I dropped the hose and ran across the lawn to the gate. There was Nappy, greedily munching on the grass he had not been able to reach through the fence. Kyle, on his feet by now, stood among the broken white boards of the fence, with his left back leg dangling. He was quivering from shock. I called the vet immediately, knowing that Kyle would have to be put to sleep, the sooner the better. In the meantime, I kept Nappy near him and stroked Kyle's long, sad face. The vet arrived with her black bag and plastic tray. Kyle's head lowered as the second needle went in, and he collapsed to the ground under the maple tree.

I called Fred, the tractor man, who arrived at dusk. He hauled Kyle's limp body up the hill to the back of the property where there is a quiet forest of cedars. We buried Kyle there. Fred used ropes to hoist the body, and Kyle's neck and head were flung backwards as the tractor's rubber tires moved slowly along the gravel driveway. The horse's lips flopped open, and my last sight of Kyle was his worn brown teeth nubs. I sprinkled red poppy seeds over his grave.

After Fred left I finished off my nightly chores. Nappy was calling for Kyle and pacing up and down the fence. He quieted down by dark, but the next morning he didn't eat his breakfast. I brushed his thick coat and picked out his hoofs, then took him for a short walk around the property. He didn't have much energy.

The week that followed Kyle's death was quiet. Some weeks are like that – no telephone calls, no visitors, no projects going on – so I just putter around. It's a time to catch up on reading, talk to my tenants and finish little jobs. I noticed that handfuls of Nappy's thick fur began to appear in the brush when I groomed him. Stress, I thought: Nappy missed his friend.

On a hot summer day the following year, Nappy collapsed in his field from a heart attack. It was over quickly, and he died with a mouthful of grass. I was with him for his last few seconds of life.

Fred came over again at dusk, and I asked him to put Nappy up on the shady hill next to Kyle. That was the only time I could not watch an animal being buried. While Fred buried Nappy, I washed the car. I did the farm chores and then read by the fire for the rest of the evening.

In the morning, I called Mum from bed as soon as I woke up.

"I have some very sad news about Nappy," I choked out.

"Oh, the dear old fellow," Mum said. "He had a wonderful time! I shall miss him, that little moose face."

Then Mum said, "Here comes Bruno – I have to go." Havel, who is a very sensitive dog, began to lick my face as Mum and I said good-bye. I petted him for a few minutes, then got up, emptied my hot water bottle and went downstairs to begin the day's chores. The Naked Necks were cackling to be fed.

How to Build a Hedgerow

BELOW THE BARNS on Glamorgan Farm, in a meadow where tall yellow and red hollyhocks bloom, is a beautifully cultivated field of allotment garden plots. These fertile black squares of earth are tended by local people, mostly older couples who live in apartment blocks. A local community group had approached me with the idea.

The meadow I donated for the allotment plots was hardened with clay (most of North Saanich sits on this yellow clay – "So hard you can make a road with it," says one of my neighbours) and full of stones. For weeks, the gardeners arrived as the sun rose, before it got too hot, and picked away at the thirty plots with hoes, mattocks and other sharp, pointed tools. They were bent over for hours in their sun hats, chopping at the hard ground, hosing it to dampen the clay, pulling out the dock weed, thistles, burdock, blackberry brambles and broom. They ripped out ivy until their hands were red and sore. They built a wooden frame around each plot, then dug trenches for the water pipes and for drainage. Green rubber hoses were neatly coiled around handmade wooden hose-racks, and the tool shed was outfitted with new hooks and a cork bulletin board with a list of all the gardeners and their telephone numbers pinned to it.

Perspiring, shirtless men of all ages spent hours in the late spring rain, shovelling out rich black topsoil from a truck until each plot was filled. Once the soil was raked smooth, the plots were ready for planting. Before long, sunflowers, artichokes, rhubarb patches, pink and purple cosmos, and rows of leafy greenery began to appear.

A man with hearing aids and a cap comes every morning at the crack of dawn to water his peas, which are bigger than anyone else's. An older couple from Poland grows rows of lush kale and huge, succulent cabbages. They sit on plastic patio chairs to eat sandwiches and drink tea from a thermos between weeding and watering sessions. A dark woman with glasses and a cape comes at dusk to plant lima beans and Brussels sprouts in wavy lines and weird-looking mounds. And one woman with a kind face plants nothing in her plot but various types of catnip; in the autumn, she dries it to make the stuffed mice she gives to the orphaned cats at the SPCA. Wild cats from the racetrack sit silently in the deep shade of the mint canopies of her plot through the hot summer months. She leaves little dishes of water and cat crunchies among the greenery.

At the other end of the meadow is a small orchard of heritage fruit trees that I planted soon after I moved to Glamorgan Farm. One of the trees, called a Lady Apple, was originally developed by Louis XIV. The apples are small, hard and red, and the French used them for decorating everything from wreaths to wigs.

One late summer day, a tall man in a straw hat came striding up the driveway. He said his name was Gavin, and he was an herb and salad gardener. He was looking for a space "to work the earth." Gavin spoke in a quiet tone, and he had a quiet face. I said he could have the orchard if he cleaned it up and mulched and pruned the fruit trees.

Gavin showed no obvious appreciation for my offer (he even complained about the noise from occasional airplanes overhead), but the next day he came back again, strolling up the driveway in his straw hat. He stood for a long while under the shade of the poplar trees and looked at the meadow. He had a rolled-up paper under his arm, which turned out to be a plan for his herb garden. He described it as a wheel, and in each spoke he would grow a different herb. Lavender would be planted in the outer rim of the wheel, edible flowers and shrubs next to that, and herbs towards the middle. In the centre would be a pond surrounded by fruit trees. He would transplant, prune and mulch the struggling trees I had already planted.

Gavin settled in and began the backbreaking work of digging up the rough clay soil. All that summer he built rockeries, mowed the field, pruned fruit trees and planted herbs. He created an enormous compost pile, which he contained with poles and a fishnet. I dumped the farm manure on the pile, and neighbours kept appearing with truckloads of grass clippings and yard waste. Soon the pile was higher than my head. It smelled sweet, like a cow's breath after it has eaten. Gavin transported the rotting compost in a blue wheelbarrow, making endless trips in the summer heat.

In the evenings Gavin could be seen in the wooded areas of the farm, bending over in the dewy grass to pick little sprigs and leaves. One day a giant bag of "Gavin's Wild Salad Greens" appeared on my doorstep. More than ten wild greens were delicately mixed together, all picked on the property. They were delicious. Gavin told me that he sold wild greens to local restaurants and hotels.

One day a man who had heard about the gardens on Glamorgan Farm offered us a truckload of heritage rose bushes that he had dug up to make room for his new house. Gavin and I decided to build a hedgerow beside the white fence that runs along Glamorgan Road. Hedgerows have many purposes. They serve as wind breaks and buffer areas between properties, and they are both privacy screens and weed controllers. They prevent soil erosion and provide a habitat for small animals and birds. Hedgerows are also wonderful to look at. Along with the heritage roses, Gavin and I decided to plant jasmine, huckleberry, wild currant, apple and plum trees, japonica, Indian plum and Saskatoon berry.

Gavin worked for weeks on the trench, chipping through the clay, pulling out rocks, carrying in buckets of his sweet-smelling compost and soil. He planted each bush carefully, watering its tender roots. He spread mulch around each plant to prevent the moisture from evaporating too quickly in the summer heat. I had a bucket of magenta poppy seeds I'd collected the previous autumn from the hundreds of poppy plants that grow in the rockeries, and I threw those in as well.

There's an interesting story behind these poppies. When I moved to Glamorgan Farm, I brought with me a load of topsoil from Ever Lasting Farm, where I'd been living. I considered the black, fertile mound part of my furniture – rich topsoil is like gold to a gardener. It had been sitting in my field for a year by that time: through the autumn, under the wispy boughs of a group of willows; through the pounding winter rains and storms; through a spring beside white-blossomed apple trees and hawthorn bushes and then among the buttercups, chicory and blackberries of summer. Fred brought over his bulldozer, and we dumped the soil around the new farm in areas where I had planned rockeries or flower beds.

When spring came to Glamorgan Farm that first year, I got a magnificent surprise. In front of all the barns, along the gravel driveway, in the rockeries and in between the squash and cabbages – everywhere I had placed the topsoil – grew forests of the most wonderful, sturdy purple poppies.

GLAMORGAN POPPIES

Watercolour by Molly Lamb Bobak

My friend Lorna has a poem called "In Moonlight." It includes a line that captures for me how much more nature knows than we do. The poem talks about "the garden going on without us." There is an ease in nature, an un-order that is meant to be. Now I wait for the purple poppies every year with immense pleasure.

So Gavin and I planted our hedgerow, and twice a week he lugged the rubber hoses across from his herb garden and watered the shrubs. By the next spring, the hedgerow reminded me of J.E.H. MacDonald's painting "The Tangled Garden."

That summer Mum came for a visit. Although her eyesight is failing, she still has the physical strength to putter around the farm. She got hold of a pair of clippers and went around snipping off overgrown weeds and dead plants from the previous season.

Exhausted by tea time, she had a bath upstairs, then changed her clothes and sat outside in the fading sun with a cup of tea and a gingersnap. "That was a great day," she sighed. "I clipped back all those invasive weeds along the fence, where that nice boy Gavin has his herb garden." My heart sank.

But the poppies managed to adjust, to root, sprout and blossom as they had always done. The following spring, we had a thick hedgerow of volunteer poppies in a thousand shades of pink and magenta. People who stopped on the road to admire them asked for seeds and our gardening secrets. Despite poor Mum's mistake, nature had truly gone on without us.

Gavin's Wild Greens Salad

(Ingredients all picked on Glamorgan Farm)

Wash and place in a large salad bowl any combination
of the following greens:

chickweed	black mustard
winter purslane	sheep sorrel
dandelion	lamb's quarters
shepherd's purse	pigweed
chicory	ox-eye daisy
land cress (two types)	

Toss with the following dressing, a recipe from family
friend and fabulous artist Joe Plaskett:

2 large cloves of garlic, crushed

a squirt of balsamic vinegar

a heaping tsp. of stone-ground mustard

5 leaves of freshly chopped basil

¼ cup of orange or peach juice

⅛ cup of flaxseed oil

ground black pepper to taste

Decorate salad with edible flowers: nasturtium,
evening primrose, bachelor's button or rose petals.

Well Placed

OCCASIONALLY, I EMBARK on a risky project on Glamorgan Farm. There are many ideas that sound good at the time, but then I lose interest or develop doubts halfway through. Every so often, however, the thing takes off without me, and that's when I say, "If it's meant to be, it will happen."

Such was the case with the decision to import two Gloucester Old Spots pigs from Oregon. These pigs are extinct in this country, according to Rare Breeds Canada, and, during a chat by the fire one evening, my friend Joan and I decided to change the face of Canadian agriculture and ship in two females. Gloucester Old Spots, with their black spots and big ears, sounded way more interesting than the normal pink pigs every hobby farmer seems to have. Joan and I had done some research, and other pigs on the threatened list were the Red Wattle and the British Lop. For poultry, it was the Hungarian

Naked Neck and the Hollywood Leghorn. We were sold!

A young female pig is called a gilt, and our first embarrass-
ment was to write to the British Gloucestershire Old Spots Pig
Breeders' Club and enthusiastically tell them that we were saving
their pig in Canada by importing two "guilts" as breeding stock.
Joan proofread our application, and she *thinks* she remembers
correcting the mistake – after all, she is a retired professor. It
must have been the Scotch. Over my second Bombay Gin martini I decided to name my pig Catherine of Oregon. Joan thought
she might name hers Joan of Pork. We didn't know a darn thing
about pigs. We had only just found out that they sweat through
their snouts and that they like their bellies rubbed. Joan is a lit-
erature expert and I am an elected local councillor. But I did
own one of the oldest farms on Vancouver Island, and I had an
empty barn available.

Joan has a lot more gumption than I do. When we sent in our
membership application to the Gloucestershire Old Spots Club
in Britain, she actually put in a note asking what they'd suggest
we learn about pigs. I expected them to write back and say, "You
cannot be part of our club if you know nothing about pigs!" but
to our delight a nice woman responded to tell us that Gloucester
Old Spots like their potatoes boiled, and that show females must
have "fourteen well-placed teats." She included a brochure about
their club, a glossy pamphlet subtitled "The rare breed with a big
future." I didn't really understand. A big future in what? Bacon?

OLD SPOTS

Pencil drawing by Bruno Bobak

Obedience pig classes at a Royal Pig Show at Temple Newsam, apparently the Gloucester Old Spots breeding capital of the planet? I'd seen some pig-obedience classes at our local Saanich fair. The pigs had to do figure eights while their handlers, mostly teenagers, used wooden canes to steer them.

Joan and I learned a lot from the brochure. "The coloured pigment [of the skin] does not show in the meat," it told us. Whew! No spotted pork chops. When we were ready to breed our gilts, a good source of semen would be the Irish champion, Rufus of Dublin, now standing at stud. ("Can't he lie down?" asked a visiting friend, with great concern.) The gilt-breeder we contacted in Oregon said that we might be able to get some good semen closer to home, from New England. I could picture our local veterinarian racing across the field, clutching a small plastic cooler full of chilled semen on ice, while Catherine of Oregon and Joan of Pork sat anxiously waiting in their bed of straw.

We'd agreed that Joan would be the pigs' primary caregiver. As we read, I said to her, "Did you know that our piggies will grow to be over six hundred pounds? What if, when you're feeding them, they charge you and crush you against the wall?"

Joan, who is a retired women's studies professor, answered sublimely, "Crushed and smothered by two six-hundred-pound sows, each with fourteen well-placed teats – what a way to go."

We established communication with Dr. Crumper, the food inspector from Agriculture Canada who had to approve my barn as a quarantine facility for a thirty-day period after the pigs arrived. We worked all week on the checklist of items to be approved. First of all, the list instructed, "All gates must be locked and posted 'No Admittance.'" The only sign I could find read "Employees Only" in big red letters. "Is that the same as 'No Admittance'?" I fretted, as I stapled one up on each gate. We were also supposed to disinfect the barn. Joan had picked up a large bottle of lemon-fresh Lysol with which we scrubbed the barn long past midnight on a frosty moonlit evening, under one bare light bulb. I got a stepladder and a paint scraper and worked off manure blobs on the wooden walls as Joan aimed the hose. How could manure get stuck twelve feet up a wall?

Joan bought herself a new pair of coveralls and new rubber boots to wear whenever she was in the barn. She'd need to dip her boots into a disinfectant foot bath before entering or leaving the barn, so we set a new red bucket and a bottle of Dettol beside the door. Joan and I hired a carpenter, Ken, to construct the actual pigpen enclosure. The final thing on the checklist was drainage.

At last the day of Dr. Crumper's visit arrived. All seemed to be going well until we got to the pig enclosure. We had neglected to ask Ken to build a holding pen to contain the pigs while they were having their blood tests, a regular procedure until the pigs had been cleared of all disease. My heart sank. But we agreed Ken would build the holding pen the next day, and Dr. Crumper would come back to inspect.

As Dr. Crumper was leaving, Joan said, "I know the pigs like their potatoes boiled, but what about other scraps?"

Dr. Crumper stopped in his tracks and looked pale. "You must *never* feed pigs scraps," he said. "In England, when they fed them scraps from the army – and those were clean scraps, believe me – as soon as the pigs defecated, thirty viruses were released in the wind." Joan and I felt like two naughty school-children as we stared at the ground.

Ken fixed the containment area, and Dr. Crumper approved it. I called the breeder in Oregon with the good news. She said she had two things to tell me. First, there would be an added expense for the green tattoo each pig had to have on her ear in order to cross the border. The tattoo was to read "U.S.A." "That's ridiculous!" snorted Joan, when I told her. "Trust that George Bush." The breeder had a more dramatic bomb to drop, too. One of the pigs had only twelve teats, she said. I was shattered, though I managed to mumble, "But are they well placed?"

In the end, Joan and I decided to call our gilts Mabel and Matilda. We chose beautiful cream-coloured letterhead with subtle block printing as our writing paper. It reads "Glamorgan Farm Old Spots." Our first choice was "The Old Spot Corral," but we thought the British might not find it amusing, and Rufus of Dublin might not want anything to do with us, should we need his donation someday.

Finally the big day came — Mabel and Matilda were to arrive in the early evening from Oregon. Their breeder and her husband were driving them up in their pickup truck. Joan and I were tense all day for fear there would be a delay at the border, a bureaucratic error in the paperwork or a new swine-disease alarm sent out at the last minute. The truck had to be disinfected before the pigs entered and then sealed. Dr. Crumper was the only one allowed to break the seal, so the unloading would be done the next morning. Joan decided to sleep over at the farm to help the pigs settle into their new home. She left her seaside cottage among the tall fir trees and came over right after supper. We sat by the fire and waited.

The breeder called from the ferry to tell us they'd made it through the border. But after twenty minutes I began to fret, since I live only five minutes from the ferry terminal. It was a dark night, teeming with a cold rain, and I looked out the big living- room window, hoping to see some sign of ferry traffic in the distance. Instead, I saw the flashing lights of our local volunteer fire department and of police cars screaming down the highway, swarming the nearest intersection. "Oh, God," I said to Joan, "they've been driving for fifteen hours and here it is raining and they don't know our signage and they've crashed the pigs! I'll drive down and check." Joan stayed by the telephone.

There were red and yellow rescue vehicles all over the road. There had indeed been a pile-up — several cars were smashed along the cement barricade separating the lanes, and a truck was being sprayed with foamy fire retardant. I parked on a dead-end street, waded through a grassy ditch and scrambled over a mangled wire fence. It was chaos. Some of the crumpled vehicles had smoke coming out of their engines, and the place smelled of burning rubber. I recognized our local fire chief. He was dressed in a yellow rubber suit and was pulling a canvas fire hose from one of the trucks.

"Gary! Gary!" I called frantically from the side of the road. "Are there any pigs involved? From Oregon?" He didn't hear me. I stood for a few intense seconds in awe at the work these emergency people do.

It was quiet driving back down dark, narrow Glamorgan Road between the hedgerows. What a relief when I pulled into the driveway. A pickup truck was parked beside the pear tree, and I saw Joan in her raincoat with a flashlight walking towards it.

Joan directed the breeder and her husband to the upper field beside the pig barn. I traipsed along behind, through the mud. Joan shone her yellow light through the truck's back window, and we finally laid eyes on what looked like two massive pink hairy slugs with large black spots. We couldn't see their burrowed heads, only the jelly-like pink bodies, round buttocks and curly tails. Our months of anticipation were over, and a new phase had begun.

We planned to hold a swearing-in for Mabel and Matilda after their thirty-day quarantine period, so that they could become truly Canadian. We made invitations and sent them to our friends. Joan knew some famous literary people from her professor days, several of whom had been awarded the Order of Canada. Mum was visiting by then, too, and she had also been appointed to the Order. Queen Elizabeth and Governor General Adrienne Clarkson had prior engagements, so it was decided that Joan's distinguished friends and Mum would hold court at the great swine swearing-in. Joan gave Mabel and Matilda a sponge bath in preparation.

Dress for the occasion was "Farm Formal," and we'd asked Order of Canada recipients to wear their medals. First to arrive was Ann Saddlemyer, a Canadian writer and Yeats scholar who had written a Piggie Oath. Canadian poet P.K. Page sent her regrets along with a welcoming poem. Mum wore jeans and a Cowichan sweater. She didn't have her medals with her (she said Dad had locked them away for safekeeping), so I made her a medal from a blue ribbon I'd won at the Saanich Fair. My bookseller friends Clive and Christine arrived, he in gumboots, black baggy shorts and a straw hat, she in a long skirt with a parasol and pearls. During the ceremony, Clive sang a country song that was full of rude noises, and Christine made an elegant speech in French. The guests stood in the deep hay as Mabel and Matilda slept in the middle of the pen. When it came time for the oath, Ann stood on a platform to read it as Joan and I took hold of one stubby, bristled leg from each pig and placed them on copies of *Winnie the Pooh*. Joan had spray-painted the barn walls, which had been recently disinfected, with slogans like "Great Pigs!" and "Unique in Canada." Following the ceremony, our guests made a procession to the house, where we sat around and drank champagne.

That night, after the chores were finished and Mum and I had had our supper, we sat outside on the lawn beside the honeysuckle bush until we felt that familiar West Coast sunset chill. Mabel and Matilda had had their supper earlier, cooked potatoes and kibble from their new red pail. It really didn't matter what nation the Gloucester Old Spots came from, I thought, because, as the saying goes, "Dogs look up to people, cats look down on people, but pigs *are* people." Mum and I went to bed, and another day had ended on Glamorgan Farm.

MABEL AND MATILDA,

the only Gloucester Old Spots pigs in Canada,
recently imported from Oregon with a combined preteen
weight of 600 pounds, and having in total 26 well-placed
teats, very cordially invite you to attend their
Canadian Swearing-In.

Please join us on February 28, Saturday,
at 10:00 A.M. for the Swearing-In Ceremony:
Performed by Order of Canada celebrities
Dr. Ann Saddlemyer — famous heritage vegetarian
author of *Becoming George* — and Molly Lamb Bobak
— famous blind war artist

Followed by a fine selection of refreshments:
❖ It's SNOUT-TASTIC yam and alfalfa pie with mud
❖ more mud with grubs ("mud à la mud" — house specialty)
❖ dirt-covered grubs topped with black soil with a hint of mud
❖ nettle roots with grit & compost with a delicate aroma of mud
❖ delicious dirt blended with loam with a mud swirl
❖ sliced apple & banana mousse with damp soil marinated in mud
❖ more mud, topped with a dollop of North Saanich
clay, layered in mud
❖ boiled potato with turnip pureed with mud with
❖ an earthy sandy tone worm in naturally filtered
muddied water (right out of the drain!)
❖ whipped carrot juice with diced mud

Proud owners "PIG MAMMA," a.k.a. Joan Coldwell, Ph.D., and
"SLOP SOW," a.k.a. Anny Scoones, councillor for North Saanich,
hope you can make this special event.

Dress: "Farm Formal"

Oath of Allegiance

As Canadian citizens, in the absence of other representatives
of Her Majesty and an Immigration Officer, it is our pleasure to
welcome Mabel and Matilda, registered Gloucester Old Spots
Pigs, to this great country of ours, renowned for its tolerance,
generosity and unique northern heritage. By introducing yet one
more thread into our vast multicultural web and rescuing your
kind from oblivion, your sponsors, Pig Mamma and Slop Sow,
are to be congratulated on their foresight and inventiveness.
We look to them to continue their care in educating you
in the path you are expected to follow – no matter where
in this vast land it may take your families.

Meanwhile, having been appointed guardians of all things
bright, beautiful and heritageneous, we – artist Molly Lamb
Bobak and author Ann Saddlemyer – ask that you swear with
cloven hoof on this well-loved book, *Winnie the Pooh*, inspired by
that great western city of Winnipeg and featuring a very
fine piglet, the following:

To honour and respect the virtues representing Canada the Good;
To promise to try not to devour the Maple Leaf, the Trillium, the
Arbutus tree and its branches, or the Garry oak and all its parts;
To acknowledge and observe the rules and boundaries of
Glamorgan Farm and its owner;
To bring up your piglets in the way of the righteous;
And to live in harmony with your fellow creatures – horse, dog,
cat, goat, duck, hen, turkey, and other farm animals – who are
bound to join you on this great Heritage Adventure.

Having thereby sworn to obey the regulations of Farm and
Country, you are now pronounced Citizens of Canada.
Welcome, and congratulations!

Dear Matilda and Mabel
I wish I were able
to cheer at your cer-e-monee.
But to my enragement
a prior engagement
prevents me from coming to tea.

As newcomers here –
my dear and my dear –
you will probably welcome some tips:
if you want to get thinner
a Maple Leaf dinner
will take the weight off of your hips.

If you need to know how
a Canadian sow
deports herself morning and night
then Emily Post
will give you the most
(and the best) information in sight.

Let us lift up our glasses
to two lovely lasses
whose pulchritude fills us with bliss.

Oink oink we rejoice
at the sounds of their voice.
Matilda and Mabel – a kiss!

—P.K. PAGE

Lost

WHENEVER MUM VISITS, we like to get up just as the sun is rising above the distant dark islands. We take our walk down to the end of Glamorgan Road, past the blackberry and rosehip hedges to a small tunnel created by the towering cedars. At the end of this trail is a lane leading to other farms in the neighbourhood. But we cut off before we reach it, following instead an overgrown path among the brambles. We crawl through an arc of Saskatoon berry, wild honeysuckle and hawthorn, step over a wet ditch and then follow a narrow deer trail through high grass to arrive at our secret meadow.

We discovered this meadow soon after I bought Glamorgan Farm. Walking through it, we came upon a magnificent sight. Standing by itself in the wild grasses was a gigantic, old pear tree, covered so thickly in little hard pears that we could barely see its branches. Because the tree was not tended, the crowded pears were bitter, but we took a bag home and Mum made chutney all afternoon. Now gathering pears from this tree is our autumn ritual.

One hot September afternoon, we set off for the amazing pear tree accompanied by Baby Alice Mary. Merlin, the smelly Nigerian Dwarf billy goat, also decided to join us. Merlin was a strange creature who'd been abandoned on Saltspring Island, roaming the country roads and scrounging in ditches. An animal control officer picked him up, and through a series of interconnections, Merlin came to Glamorgan Farm.

Merlin was quite a sight when he arrived. His coat was a filthy tangled mat of coarse white hair. He had a rotund stomach and very short legs, one of them trembling and withered. His nervous darting eyes were like marbles and his beard was thick and pungent, full of communities of gnats and midges. He also had a lovely set of curled horns. When he walked, he looked like a child's pull toy.

Merlin had a mind of his own, too. He always knew what he wanted. When he arrived at the farm in the animal control van, we had to carry him to the chicken barn, where I'd made him a hay bed with the Naked Necks. The chickens were rather offended, though – probably by the smell – and for days Merlin sat in that dark barn among the cobwebs and wouldn't come out.

Then he met Baby Alice Mary. She would go into the chicken barn when I wasn't watching to scrounge for fresh eggs. I'd catch

MERLIN IN THE CHICKEN BARN

Watercolour by Molly Lamb Bobak

her sometimes with her paws on the ledges and her big head in the nests. One afternoon she swaggered out of the barn licking delicious orange yolk off her lips, with Merlin following close behind. He hobbled to keep up and bleated if Alice Mary got too far ahead. When she heard him, she'd stop to wait.

After a while Merlin began coming onto the porch and sleeping in the extra dog basket. I gave him an old Mexican blanket, and the porch soon began to smell of billy goat. Over time, Merlin worked up the courage to enter the house with Alice Mary. He began to eat dog food from her dish, and he even climbed up on the couch with her so we could all watch *The Air Farce* together. Mum did a drawing of us.

Merlin was part of the household after that. If he got left outside, he would bang his horns on the door until I let him in. He came on walks with Alice Mary and me, although this took forever because he was so slow. It wasn't just his legs. He was short of breath, and if we went too fast he would heave into a violent coughing fit. He retained his pungent odour, since he would never let me touch him.

One day an SPCA officer on his neighbourhood rounds stopped us in the racetrack field. He got out of his van looking very official. "Do you have a licence for these dogs, and what is that?" he said. He pointed to Merlin, who was hobbling along with a hawthorn branch in his mouth.

"That's a billy dog," I said, very matter of fact. I showed him

Alice Mary's tags and then added, "In North Saanich we don't licence billy dogs."

The officer looked puzzled as he returned to his van.

I knew the old pear tree was much too far for Merlin to walk, but he insisted on following along with Mum and me and Baby Alice Mary. By the time we reached the shady trail at the end of the road, Merlin had to lie down and rest his tired leg. We resigned ourselves to a long afternoon.

When we reached the low arc of brambles leading to the meadow, we had to stop again, because Merlin had a coughing fit. Alice Mary lay in the dry grass beside him. Mum and I picked a few blackberries. When he was ready, we continued on our mission. Alice Mary had a wade in the pond while Merlin nibbled a few tender willow shoots on the muddy shore. Finally, we reached our magnificent tree, and Mum and I filled our bag with pears. Merlin ate one himself, his mouth going neatly from side to side. He seemed to blend in perfectly with his surroundings.

We set off for home, lugging our heavy bag of pears for chutney. Mum was looking forward to a cup of tea and a bath. I still had to gather the eggs and feed the cows. Then we planned to light the fire and entertain ourselves with some Russian history.

"I wonder who will overthrow Sophia?" Mum asked, referring to our nightly reading sessions of *Peter the Great*.

"Maybe we should watch the battle scene in *War and Peace* instead," I suggested.

"Oh, that Prince Andrei makes me swoon," answered Mum.

Mum and I were distracted from our lazy stroll by a sudden loud orchestration of catchy American tunes. "In the Mood," "Camptown Races" and "Oh, What a Beautiful Morning" filled the air, blaring from a posse of shiny mobile homes, each with a speaker mounted on the cab, heading in a slow procession down Glamorgan Road. Their licence plates read "Family Coach Clubs of America," and each RV was towing a small car.

Men in oversized mesh tractor hats and women with coiffed hair cheerily waved good-bye to one another. They had been parked for the weekend at Sandown, enjoying their annual jamboree.

Mum put the kettle on when we got back and sat down to core the pears. I rinsed out some canning jars. Baby Alice Mary flopped herself down in her basket. I continued about my chores and Mum put the pear chutney on for its long simmer. It wasn't until then that we noticed Merlin was absent. He hadn't returned home with us along the road – or had he? Our blissful time in the meadow, followed by the blow-horn tunes, had put us into a rather distracted state, and neither Mum nor I could recall when we had last seen him.

I did a walk around the farm, but Merlin was nowhere to be found. Mum had her bath while I retraced our afternoon route, calling Merlin's name and hoping to hear his sharp,

single-pitched bleat in return. No luck. I checked the ditches along Glamorgan Road – nothing. By now I was beginning to be a little anxious. Where could Merlin have gone?

Mum had set out bread and made a big salad from the garden, while I prepared a boletus mushroom Naked Neck omelette. Boletuses are the Jane Russells of mushrooms. They have golden, spongy bottoms and slimy amber caps and grow under the Garry oaks on cool, damp nights.

Our entire dinner conversation revolved around Merlin.

"I hope he hasn't fallen down an abandoned well," Mum said. "He's so old."

"Maybe he got disoriented and took a wrong turn," I

theorized. "Perhaps we should take a drive around the neighbourhood."

So after supper, that's what we did. We stopped to ask a few people out for their evening walk, "Have you seen a short, shy, hairy billy dog with a bad smell and a stained yellow beard, walking with a limp? He may look confused." But nobody had seen Merlin.

Mum and I were too worried by dusk to be able to concentrate on either *Peter the Great* or *War and Peace*. So we decided to walk down Glamorgan Road to the trail in the last sliver of light before bed.

An evening breeze rustled the turning leaves of the poplar trees along the driveway. Without warning, from around the barrel of petunias at the end of the drive came Merlin, doing a rather brisk trot. He was bleating anxiously. Ignoring Mum and me, and not even pausing to greet Alice Mary, he made a beeline for the porch. By the time we got there, Merlin was sitting in his basket on his Mexican blanket, his withered leg twitching over the edge.

Calm had returned to Glamorgan Farm. Merlin ate a dog biscuit, his crusty eyelids heavy, and soon he and Alice Mary were both asleep in their beds.

The Death of Merlin

DECEMBER IS A quiet time on the farm. The cows lie in the barn on their beds of thick hay, chewing their cud as the steam rises from their warm skin. The chickens line up on the door ledge, looking out at their long muddy pen. Whenever there's a break in the weather, I dig worms for them. I feed them more corn in these bleak wet months too, and fluff up the hay in their nests every day. Their nests are used mainly for napping, since egg production drops dramatically at this time of year. The horses wear special waterproof blankets, and I tend their hoofs with a copper solution to prevent hoof rot from the constant moisture.

My winter chores consist mainly of chopping wood and towelling off wet animals. Not too much grows in the garden – a little kale, maybe, and perhaps some chard. Hanging Christmas lights on the shrubs, trees and barns always provides a little excitement in these long, dripping, steel-grey days. I fling coloured strings of lights randomly on the two pear trees near the house, and yards of larger white lights are placed in neat loops among the branches of the poplar trees along the driveway. As soon as the Christmas mandarin oranges are available at the store, I start putting peels in the wood stove in the kitchen, and a wonderful musky smell wafts through the house as the peels smoulder. I plant paperwhite bulbs in clay pots on the windowsill, watching them grow into tall, delicate white flowers. One of my neighbours had given me a wreath she makes from pine cones, acorns and dried rosehips, all tied together with a gold ribbon, and I put it up each year.

I cook a turkey for Christmas dinner, of course, and bake a big fresh squash from the garden. For dessert I bring out a few jars of the ginger pears I bottled in the early autumn. Mum always sends a heavy, round plum cake, and I pour the pears with a little brandy onto the cake and light the whole thing on fire. It's delicious. Sometimes my tenants join me, and I give them warm socks and candles as presents, in case the power goes off some blustery night.

One year, however, I found myself alone on Christmas Eve. It had been a damp day, mild and soft. The drizzle hung in the air, and at dusk the Christmas lights were muted in the mist. I served hot bran mash with apple and molasses to the horses, and a dinner of grainy bread, taco chips and raisins to the chickens and ducks. The cows were enjoying a bale of sweet alfalfa hay. I lit the fire when I got back to the house, then put a stew on the stove to simmer in Gran's white enamel pot. After a hot bath, I put on my flannelette nightie and sat by the fire. The dogs were fast asleep among the pillows on the sofa, and Merlin had joined them. Goats seem to dislike rain more than any other farm animal.

My little Christmas tree sat at the end of the sofa. There were a few decorations hanging from its spindly branches – some gold glass angels Mum and I had picked up in Prague and a few red balls. Under the tree were some "tokens," as Mum called them, that I'd received in the mail. I had already put her plum cake and her annual batch of Turkish delight in the fridge. Dad had wrapped the presents in all sorts of recycled material – a pink plastic pantyhose-bag tied with a piece of green raffia, an outdated opera poster announcing Verdi's *Aida* tied with fishing line. My parents always send me interesting and useful items: a pair of blue woollen mittens knitted by my old grade-two teacher, who sells them at the Saturday market in Fredericton; a T-shirt emblazoned with Mum's colourful painting of a boat race on the Saint John River; a full video set of *Pride and Prejudice* and, of course, treats for the dogs and cans of tuna for all the farm kitties.

Once the presents were opened and the wrapping folded and put away, I sat down to eat my stew. Suddenly Merlin let out a loud bleat – a sharp, panicked cry. He looked around him and then took a violent tumble from the sofa, his curled horns hook-

ing onto the tree. Baby Alice Mary and Havel leapt up in surprise. Merlin was flopping around on the floor, his yellow eyes
wide open, his short legs in the air. It was shocking. Then, just
as suddenly, he was motionless. His rotund body lay very still on
its side. The dogs cautiously sniffed him over.

My tree and its decorations were scattered across the floor,
and the lamp with the pink silk shade had toppled too. I covered
Merlin with a blanket, then tidied up the mess. Keeping busy
seemed to calm me after the traumatic event, but the problem
still remained – Merlin was lying dead in the middle of the living room floor, and it was Christmas Eve.

Outside it was dark and raining. "What should I do?" I asked
the dogs, who sat staring first at Merlin, then up at me. Was
Merlin really dead? What if he was just in some sort of goat
coma? I pulled the blanket away from his face to see his yellow
marble eyes, still wide open, and his rough pink tongue jutting
out from between a tiny, neat set of teeth. "So that's what goats'
teeth look like," I remember thinking.

Within the hour, I'd sadly accepted that Merlin's time had
come. I decided to dig a hole under the plum tree as a temporary
burial place. I was about to clip off a strand of his thick stained
beard when it hit me that Merlin would not have liked that.

I took the stew off the stove, damped down the fire and went
to the shed for the shovel. It was a mild night, and I grew hot
from digging up the soft clay. Once I had a big enough hole, I

went back into the house to wrap Merlin in his blue and black Mexican blanket. I carried him outside, but he was heavy for being so short. I had to get the wheelbarrow to wheel him to his grave. Baby Alice Mary, Havel, Annabelle the barn cat and a few wild ducks gathered around. Although I would like to think they were there to pay their last respects, I think they were just curious about all the activity.

The grave I'd dug was quite shallow, since the ground deeper down is rocky and hard. I'd call Fred on Boxing Day to dig me a deeper hole. For now I laid Merlin in his grave and put a few shovelfuls of dirt over him, along with some cedar boughs and a few sprigs of holly. If I had known what sort of prayer to say over a dead Nigerian Dwarf goat, I would have said one, but instead I just said good-bye.

It was close to midnight, and I decided to walk to the church down the road for the midnight Christmas service. I changed my clothes, gave the dogs a cookie, and turned out the lights. Then I set off over the fields in the rain for the historic shake-and-shingle church at the bottom of the hill.

I sat in the back row with an Italian family who could not speak English – I was relieved. The church was warm and decorated with holly tied with red velvet ribbons. The minister wore white robes with green trim. We sang carols, and I thought of Merlin and the years he'd enjoyed on Glamorgan Farm. I remembered the terribly tense day he became lost in the pear orchard and the time he'd climbed on top of a real estate agent's new red Mercedes and banged with his beautiful horns until he dented the roof. Whenever an animal dies on Glamorgan Farm, I wish I had a faith that would help ease the loss. But I don't. I knew Merlin was simply lying in the cold ground, waiting to be feasted on by little creepy-crawlies – a magnificent Christmas Eve dinner for the life that goes on beneath our feet.

When I arrived back at the farm, the house was dark and silent. The dogs greeted me in the warm kitchen. I sat down to dry out by the stove and ate Mum's plum cake – the whole thing!

H.D.

THE STORY OF H.D. began when a tall teenager drove up to Glamorgan Farm in a new truck. Andy studied computers at a local college, but to make extra money, he raised mice and rats and sold them to pet stores. He was desperate to find a temporary place to keep them – a small space, anything would do, and he guaranteed that the rodents would be secured in their racks and that he would pay his rent on time. The rats and mice wouldn't smell, he said, because he had a good ventilation system.

I had a shack beside the house that I'd been planning to tear down, so I let Andy use it for his rodents. He came twice a week and spent the day quietly cleaning the cages. As promised, he always paid his rent on time. He regularly swept the concrete in front of the shack and always coiled up the garden hose when he was finished with it. One day I had a moment to talk to him. We sat for a while on the lawn, and that's when he told me that he sold the rats and mice as snake food. After that day, I couldn't walk by the shack without thinking how cruel fate can be.

One grey afternoon after I had finished the chores and was walking back to the house, I noticed a white speck on the lawn. Kitty was playing with it and tossing it in the air. As I approached, I could see that the speck was a white mouse, crouching stunned in the grass, its tiny red eyes half closed.

"What a brave mouse," I thought, "to make a break for it from that shack." (Which was beginning to smell, after all.) "Any creature with such courage deserves a chance." And so I picked up the mouse, placed her in a deep bucket and found a safe place for her in the house. I christened her Houdini: H.D. for short.

The next weekend I drove to a local pet store to buy some supplies for H.D. I picked out a kit called "Safari Adventure," a cage to be assembled of wheels and tunnels and ladders (the other kit, "Space Odyssey," consisted of flying saucers and planets and a replica of a NASA space shuttle); some mouse food, which looked like sunflower seeds and corn; a water bottle and some pine sawdust for H.D.'s bedding. How silly it was to be saving mice on a farm, I thought as I paid the exorbitant price. But that didn't stop me.

As coincidence would have it, as I was leaving with my armload of supplies, Andy came in with a rack of mice – he obviously had a contract with the store. I wondered if he had realized that he was missing a mouse.

"Hi," he said in his usual cheery manner. "Buying up the store?"

"Just stocking up," I mumbled, head down and shoving the bag into my armpit. What would he have thought if he'd seen the Safari kit? I shuffled awkwardly past the fish tanks and racks of colourful dog leashes while smiling Andy collected his fee from the clerk.

Back home in the bedroom, H.D. was waiting expectantly in her bucket. Before doing anything else, I had to put the Safari Adventure together. It came with an array of wires and clips, and the instructions were in Spanish. Lacking in patience (but not frustration), I stuck the whole thing together with electrical tape.

The mouse water bottle broke when I tried to shove it into the cage, so I gave H.D. a dish for her water. She had another dish for her corn and seeds. Even though I had put the cage's wheel on upside-down by mistake, she loved it, and she ran around it as fast as her legs would take her. But what she loved the most was the ladder that led up to the tunnel that led to a sleeping area. I put some Kleenex in there, because I thought she might be cold. I thought she might like to chew on something natural, so I picked her some apple leaves. I gave her some duck feathers to lie in, and a stale muffin as a treat. I placed her cage on the windowsill in the living room beside the finches, Peter and Robert, and Pip the canary. After that, I left her alone, satisfied that she had now been given a fair chance at living a life with purpose.

By the time I returned the next morning to H.D.'s cage to fill her water dish, she had constructed a magnificent bedroom. She had carried all the leaves and feathers up the ladder and made herself a large, deep nest. She had put a few seeds in there, too, and eaten her muffin. She was curled into a ball in her nest, sound asleep, exhausted from the hard work of taking care of her home. I certainly knew how she felt.

Blue-Ribbon Jerseys

I FIRST MET GEORGE and Lillian Plummer when I bought a hundred bales of hay from them a year or two ago. They live up the road on a hill surrounded by maple trees. Their house overlooks their two-hundred-acre farm, on which they run a herd of mellow, brown furry cattle. The cows are a picture of bliss, chewing their cud in the shade of a great leafy tree on a warm day, lush, cool grass all around them. George keeps his cows indoors all winter, so when they are let out in the spring they have huge dried clumps of manure hanging from their loins and jowls. A few days in the field takes care of that. From the Plummers' back porch, where a visitor can sit under the lilacs and wisteria with a glass of homemade grape juice and a piece of Lillian's delicious lemon sponge cake, you can see dots of houses separated by hedgerows and trees, the clutter of new houses on Cloake Hill and, beyond all that, the dark hills of the Gulf Islands.

Both of the Plummers are close to ninety years old. Lillian went to school in North Saanich in her early teens. George moved to North Saanich from Saskatchewan, and in his early years here he helped farm oats on Glamorgan Farm. Lillian remembers Glamorgan from her school years, when her best friend was Dorothy Holder, the daughter of the herdsman there. Dorothy and her parents lived in the log house I live in now, Lillian told me, and the owner of Glamorgan Farm, Sam Matson, lived in a stone house up the road. This was before World War II, when part of the farm was expropriated for the airport. Sam Matson owned a prize herd of Jersey cows that he showed at the Saanich Fair, always taking home the blue ribbons. He imported his prize cows from England.

I invited George and Lillian to tea so that I could ask them more questions about Glamorgan Farm. It was a blustery April afternoon – a good day for tea by the fire. I put fresh tulips on the table and filled a jug with milk. Then I set out cups and saucers from Gran's old willow pattern. Peak Frean gingersnaps and shortbread from the Deep Cove Store completed the spread. (I sometimes feel guilty that my generation doesn't bake much. I do regret never learning from Mum how to make bread – she still makes it every week – but it takes so much patience, and the yeast procedure seems so precise! And oh, all that flour all over the counter, and how to clean the rolling pin? I try to make up for my modern laziness by hanging my wash on the clothesline to dry, scrubbing the kitchen floor on my knees, and bottling massive amounts of pears in the fall.)

At two o'clock, the Plummers drove up, looking quite dapper. The dogs greeted them, tails wagging, tongues hanging out. Kitty was more aloof, lolling beside the clay pots of geraniums. George took Lillian's arm, and they made their way slowly across the gravel driveway. George is wiry and stiff, probably from so many years of farming. He has what a friend of mine would call "an open face." That afternoon he wore a big smile and his white hair was combed back in a peak. Lillian wore a red sweater of the type that only a good, strong farm woman could knit.

Once they were settled in their chairs, tea in hand, we got down to business.

"What's it like to come back to Dorothy's house?" I asked Lillian.

She started right in. "Dorothy and I used to ride our bikes to school. The schoolhouse was where the airport terminal is now. After school we came back here. Dorothy's mother was always in the milking shed churning butter, because Mr. Matson kept these Jersey cows. I remember that the butter was always rancid, though; I think the churn wasn't cleaned properly."

After a bite of gingersnap, Lillian continued. "I used to sleep over with Dorothy upstairs in a little bedroom."

I started to offer to take Lillian up to my room, but then I remembered how untidy it was with my farm clothes, books, legal documents I'd been reading on how to achieve farm status, and a jar of dying daffodils. I would extend the invitation another day.

"Tell me about Mr. Matson," I asked them both. Their eyes lit up.

"Well," said George, leaning back in his chair, "he was a character. He was creative, into all sorts of things. And he was well-liked; nobody had a bad word to say about him."

Lillian nodded. "Sam Matson started the bus line, he owned *The Daily Colonist* newspaper, and he started the ferry service to the Gulf Islands. He also built the Royal Theatre. His wife refused to come out here to the farm, so she continued to live in town. That big barn at the back of the property was the Jersey show barn, and Dorothy's father had to give the Jerseys special attention – all of the cows had soft mats to lie on."

"Tell about Miss Bowles," George interrupted with a jovial grin.

"Oh, yes, Miss Bowles," said Lillian. "Miss Bowles lived with her mother, and she met Sam at a cattle auction. The story is that she couldn't afford a small Jersey herd, so Sam helped her out. Before long he had built her a little house next to his" (the house still stands, and today the North Saanich municipal yard separates it from the Legion Hall) "and then *her* cows beat his at the fair!"

We all had a chuckle over that. Then Lillian added, "Dorothy's

father, Mr. Holder, didn't like Miss Bowles. She took the gas-
oline that the government allowed for farm use and put it in
her car!"

Times have not changed so much, I thought to myself. One
of the benefits of having "farm status" today, apart from paying
lower taxes, is that you're allowed "purple gas" for farm machin-
ery use. Lots of hobby farmers use it in their four-by-fours when
they drive into Victoria to their office jobs.

George and Lillian and I went on to discuss some of the many
rumours that abound about Sam Matson. Matson was friends
with the Dunsmuirs, the famous Vancouver Island coal-mining
family, and he was their bookkeeper, too. When Mr. Dunsmuir
died, Sam Matson continued to look after Mrs. Dunsmuir's
books – and also, some say, Mrs. Dunsmuir herself. A terrible
bovine disease called brucellosis, supposedly akin to "milk fever,"
crippled Matson's Jerseys when it hit Vancouver Island. Sam's
herd was wiped out. According to George Plummer, a neighbour found Sam dead in his bedroom one evening in 1931. The
local oldtimers said it was suicide. Miss Bowles tried to take
over Glamorgan Farm by putting locks on the gates, but loyal
Mr. Holder had them removed. Had Sam Matson promised her
the farm? Nobody knows.

Today Miss Bowles's house is sinking into the dirt and the
brambles are slowly grabbing hold of it, latching onto the paned
windows and climbing right up to the lightning rods. I am think-

ing about having a couple of Jersey cows on Glamorgan Farm, just for tradition.

George chuckled as he got up to leave and, taking Lillian's arm, he said, "Yup, Jersey cows give the best cream."

"Just keep your churn cleaned," said Lillian.

The Russian Diaries

I

ODDLY ENOUGH, it was a strange experience in Belarus that led me to buy Glamorgan Farm. Since I was a little girl, I have had an unexplainable fascination with Russia. I would look at pictures of the Kremlin in my parents' books with awe. I could never get those images out of my head: gold and blue onion domes, red brick towers, and peasants growing cabbages and drinking tea from silver samovars. I yearned to be a factory worker or a peasant. I was cheering for the Russians in the space race; their spaceship was so much more interesting. The Apollo was a dull triangle, but the Sputnik was round, with interesting spiny arms. I wrote in my diary that it looked like a kohlrabi, one of the vegetables that Dad grew in his garden.

My deep interest in Russia continued into adulthood, and in 1996 I journeyed to Minsk. Belarus is a lush country wedged between Poland and Russia. Formerly part of the Soviet Union, it is still very much under the Communist system. It was severely contaminated by the Chernobyl nuclear-plant accident. I visited there because I had made contact in Minsk with a woman named Nonna.

Nonna taught English at the Minsk language college, and I met her the summer she accompanied a group of six Belarusian children to Victoria. The children, who were ill from the Chernobyl accident, were to spend the summer with host families in order to improve their health. I took them riding one afternoon. Nonna sat in the shade in the garden while the children brushed the horses and then mounted them for a short riding lesson.

Six months after that visit, I wrote to Nonna in Minsk, and six months after that, I had a reply on a card of brown paper, inviting me to visit her in Belarus. It was a joyous, hopeful time there, she said. The Wall had fallen some years before, and the Cold War was over.

I flew first to Frankfurt, then on to Minsk. As we were coming in to land, we flew over the famous marshes and birch forests I had read so much about. "I made it!" I thought with a rush of emotion as the jet's wheels hit the runway. The terminal was rundown. Rebar protruded from the crumbling cement, and the inside of the building was dim, lit by bare light bulbs hanging from the ceiling. Broken chairs lay along a hallway that needed a good sweep. A tired-looking blonde KGB woman sat in a ply-

РЭСПУБЛІКА   REPUBLIC OF
БЕЛАРУСЬ   BELARUS

ВІЗА   VISA   **V**

№ 0485020

Прозвішча, імя
Name, surname   *SCOONES*

Пашпарт №
Passport No   *VN 883157*

Тып візы / Type of visa

А	С	Г	П	Т	В	Дз	Тр	Ж

Колькасць уездаў / Number of entries

1	2	3	шматразовая multiple

Разам едуць   чалавек
Accompanied by   people

Сэпраўдная да
Valid until   *17. 01. 97*

Тэрмін знаходжання   дзен кожны раз
Maximum stay of   *6*   days each time

Дата выдачы
Date of issue   *11. 01. 97*

Подпіс і пячаць
Signature and stamp

This passport contains 24 pages.
Ce passeport contient 24 pages.

Anny's Visa for Belarus

wood booth, wearing pink lipstick and a tight blue uniform with two gold and red stars on the jacket. She solemnly stamped my visa and then said, in a thick, Russian-spy accent, "Now you give me one hundred American dollars." So I did. I had brought all kinds of gifts as well – Rogers' chocolates, Murchie's coffee, B.C. smoked salmon and sweet-smelling shampoos. Nonna was there in her rusted Lada as I went outside into the bright sun.

Nonna and her husband and her mother, as did all Belarusians in the city, lived in an imposing grey apartment block. A special feast had been prepared for me in their small flat: pickles, radish salad, meatballs, black bread, potatoes, fried white fish and glasses of a very sweet plum drink. I had brought a bottle of B.C. wine, but Nonna spat out her first mouthful in disgust – "Too sour!" – and poured the rest down the sink. I shared around some Rogers' chocolates after the meal, and they met with more success. Nonna's husband became very excited when we talked about the Canada/Russia hockey series of 1972. He leapt up and down from the table, re-enacting the final game, with Nonna translating as fast as she could.

After dinner Nonna took me for a walk in a nearby park. People were strolling along the pathways or reading on stone benches. There were many statues among the shrubs and along the river that flowed through the park. Nonna explained that they depicted Belarusian war heroes and poets.

The buildings of Minsk were solid blocks painted in yellows

and greens, with white balconies and ornate railings. The beige KGB building took up two full city blocks. As we walked past, a man in a uniform skipped as lightly as a ballet dancer up the marble steps, a gun on his hip. Nonna said, "KGB do not like foreigners – do not speak. Keep your head down," but I couldn't keep my eyes off the man disappearing behind the heavy oak doors.

Many of the people I met in Belarus had scars on their throats – almost one person in every family. That was because so many Belarusians had developed thyroid cancer after the Chernobyl accident. A few days into my visit, I asked Nonna if I could meet some of the children who had survived Chernobyl. Nonna asked at the local hospital, but the doctor there refused, saying, "These children are not in a museum." Suddenly I felt silly, and I questioned why I had wanted to meet the children. What could I possibly have done for them?

From the time I was small, I've been preoccupied with the idea of orphans. Perhaps it comes from the times my parents left me in what Mum called a "children's hotel" when they went off on painting trips. I'm not sure if this was a boarding school or an orphanage, but I remember one little girl told me that she didn't have any parents and this place was her home. Her words never left me. I considered my large collection of troll dolls as orphans needing my care.

I had mentioned to Nonna my interest in visiting an orphanage in Minsk. She knew Nina, the woman who ran Orphanage

Number Seven, so she arranged for us to go there. The orphanage was a few miles out of town, in a grotty suburb among appliance factories and concrete office buildings that each had a hammer and sickle imprinted on the front. To get there, we took a smoky trolley bus through the grey streets.

The yellow brick orphanage sat at the top of a hill. We went around to the back entrance, where a group of curious young girls had gathered on the crumbling cement steps. They stood shyly, observing us and smiling. They wore dresses with Oriental writing on the sleeves, and each had a bow in her hair. There was a boy with them, too, not so shy, in baggy jeans, his head shaved and a rash on his smiling face. A woman with dyed red hair, a tight green miniskirt and an orange chiffon blouse materialized in the doorway, joined by two women doctors dressed in white smocks. All three greeted us with affection. The woman in the miniskirt was Nina, who ran the orphanage.

Nina led us into a dark hallway with a stone floor. The walls were painted turquoise, and the place smelled mildly of disinfectant. The not-so-shy boy – his name was Dima, Nina said – followed us inside, grinning and chatting in Belarusian. She finally convinced him to go away, but the group of little girls stayed in their cluster. When I asked about the writing on their dresses, Nina explained that the dresses had been donated by a Japanese town.

In a small medical room down the hall, a white tablecloth

had been laid over the examining table. Orange teacups were set out on it, along with a bowl of sugar and a box that held a sizeable jam cake. After some cake and instant coffee, out came the vodka for a toast to my visit.

I wanted to do something for the children at the orphanage, and I promised to return with some supplies as soon as I could. I thought to myself that I would collect clothing and toys and school supplies at home and bring it all back. Nina said that I could stay in a spare room at the orphanage and help out in the classrooms. After tea, she showed us around. The children kept what little clothing they had in closets in the hallway. The bathrooms had rows of chipped white sinks. A German company had recently donated soap and shampoo, but Nina said supplies were running out. When I saw the orderly rows of beds covered in white duvets, my childhood came flooding back, and I pictured a troll in each small bed.

Nina and the two doctors walked us back to the entrance. There was Dima, waiting for us on the steps. I took his photograph, and when I got home I sent him some wool socks along with a copy of the picture.

II

Two years later, I returned to Minsk with a load of cargo – hockey bags stuffed with donated clothing, shampoo, toys, and school and medical supplies collected from kind people in

North Saanich and the Victoria area. My friends and I had spent long winter evenings on the floor by the fire, sorting supplies and packing the bags. One friend, a retired seamstress, had sewn two hundred little bags with drawstrings, and we packed each one with surprises for the children at the orphanage – soaps, a toy truck, a chocolate bar, a comb, coloured pencils. It was a strange feeling, taking that massive amount of cargo from my living room to the North Saanich airport, knowing it would meet me three days later in Belarus. My friend Susan gave me a beautiful diary with a silver cover and handmade paper pages so that I could record my trip.

As before, the jet from Frankfurt landed on the runway in the woods outside Minsk. There was snow on the ground, and the forests looked black. The steps up to the terminal were still crumbling. The same broken plastic chairs sat in the same grey hallway. The very same KGB agent sat in her plywood booth, stamping the visas of wealthy Belarusian men in fur hats who had been away on shopping trips to Germany.

The agent gave me a look of disgust after checking over my papers, then said in her broken English, "Give me two hundred American dollars." That was double what I'd paid two years before – capitalism at work! I handed over the money. She counted it, put it in her breast pocket, stamped my passport and gestured with her hand for me to move along.

I went outside to the parking lot. There was Nonna, looking sad and tired in a brown coat and rubber boots. It was freezing. We hugged, and then she introduced me to Igor, our driver, who had a van to pick up the cargo. We bundled into the vehicle, which was so rusty that I could see the road through the floor. But when we reached the cargo pick-up area at the other end of the terminal, we were told to come back the next day. Nonna sighed and said, "Such is our people now." As we drove into Minsk, I could see cold Belarusians huddled in small groups at the trolley stops, wrapped in dark coats and holding their shopping bags.

Nina was there to greet us at the orphanage. She led me down the cold stone hallway and unlocked a door at the end. Nonna followed. The room had beige and gold wallpaper and a flickering fluorescent light. There was a small cot, covered with clean white sheets, and a broken Arborite coffee table on which a jar of pickles and sliced baloney sat waiting to be eaten. A locked Plexiglas cabinet stood full of papers, and an orange swag lamp with no bulb in it hung from a cord. There was one dark window with bars over the glass.

Nonna agreed to come back in the morning with Igor. After everyone had left, I flopped down on the cot. Here I was back at the orphanage, and I couldn't hear a sound. I ate a pickle and some baloney and wrote in my silver-covered journal. Later, in a small closet, I discovered the filthiest toilet I had ever seen. In a tiny sink, one rusted tap ran a trickle of cold water.

The next morning I woke to children's voices. I washed in the dirty sink, and Nina showed up eventually with a plate of black bread and some pickled fish. She took some yellowed paper from the Plexiglas cabinet, then left again. Nonna came in soon after. Igor was waiting in his van outside. At the airport, Nonna and I stood in line for half an hour before a woman finally gave us directions to the foreign cargo pick-up area. Back to the van we traipsed, and Igor drove us out into the bleakness.

We drove for quite a while, turning down snowy roads here and there until we came to a barbed-wire fence. Two soldiers in long grey coats and fur hats with flaps stood guarding a small shack. Nonna and Igor exchanged words with them, then more words. Nonna's voice sounded tense. Finally she told me to hand over my passport, which I did, and Igor drove through the gate. We continued past several cement bunkers surrounded by more barbed wire. The sky was white, and there was lots of snow. It would have been beautiful, like a Tolstoy novel with a troika in the woods, had it not been for the cement and the wire.

For the next six hours, we went from office to office to office, trying to locate the cargo I had sent from Canada. I filled out form after form about the contents and the value and about what I was doing in Belarus. We were followed everywhere by a skinny military man with a pimply face. He finally took us down to a basement office hazy with cigarette smoke. By then, I had anxiously consumed an entire package of cherry cough drops.

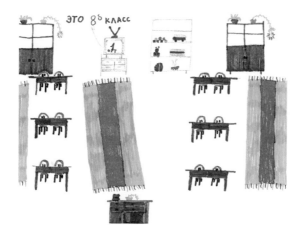

CLASSROOM, MINSK ORPHANAGE

By Dima, age 7

A burly man sat behind a solid wooden desk, smoking. He wore a bright blue uniform decorated with gold medals. We spent the next three hours there, as the man repeated over and over, with Nonna translating, "What is in the cargo? What is the value? Where are you taking it?" It was past ridiculous. Nonna kept whispering that the man probably wanted the cargo for himself or to sell on the black market. Finally, the official told us he would release the cargo for two thousand American dollars. I refused. And then I made the decision to leave.

Nonna and the man had a heated exchange, and suddenly she turned pale. Back in the van she whispered to me, "He threatened to imprison me for keeping a foreigner." That was all she said all the way back to the orphanage, through the cement bunker field and the guarded gate, down the snowy birch-treed motorway and the gloomy suburbs where factories spewed black smoke into the winter air. Nonna walked me to my room, then offered some final words as she departed: "Stay in here. Nina will bring you your meals. We must keep the door locked." As she left, I heard her lock the door from the other side. Nina had left a bottle of vodka, some boiled cabbage and more baloney on the table. That night I slept with my clothes on.

Nine days went by. Nina came at mealtimes with vodka, bread, baloney or salted fish, pickles or cabbage, and sometimes a cooked potato, but she rarely spoke, and something told me not to, either – besides, she could barely speak English. I wasn't really scared, just sort of numb. I could hear children's voices echoing in the hall as she set the tray down with the door ajar; they kept me feeling that everything was still real. I began to lose track of time. One night as I was sitting on the floor, I began counting the rings on the surface of the coffee table. After that I counted them every day, to make sure they were still there. I began to forget about North Saanich. I began to forget about Mum and my friends, and I began to forget about myself. Objects took on an exaggerated appearance. The most beautiful things in the beige room were the vodka bottles with their blue tint, sitting on the windowsill. I'd lined them up there. The labels were elegant and simple, and each bottle was slightly different. My pen ran out of ink, so I couldn't write any more in my diary.

One night a little voice came to me. "Everything will be okay," it said. It seemed to be a good voice, something that would help me, and I was so tired that I allowed it to take over. But the little voice was not intrusive. It was gentle and positive and seemed to be speaking the truth. I thought it must be what some people called God.

And then came the day that Nonna and Nina unlocked the door to take me to the airport. I picked up my bag and my ticket, checked my passport, took one of the vodka bottles from the windowsill and tucked it into my bag. I followed them down the cold, dark hall to the big door at the end. As we approached, Nina said, "Somebody wants to see you," and there stood Dima, much taller, grinning from ear to ear. I wished I could take him home to North Saanich, but instead, I gave him a package of mints from my bag. He stood holding them as we went outside onto the brown ice, and there was Igor in the rusted van.

As I went though security at the airport, a youthful guard smiled. "Canada? I visit one day. Do you fish for salmon? Do you know Wayne Gretzky?" His comrades laughed and gathered around in curiosity.

At the shiny new Frankfurt airport, where my plane was delayed for thirty-six hours, I had a shower and finally changed my clothes. I waited in various lounges for my flight to be called, observing the chic Europeans smoking strong French cigarettes and drinking espressos.

It was a damp, grey day when I got off the plane in North Saanich. I could smell the sea, and I knew that in moments I would be home. I took the familiar maroon Empress taxi back to Ever Lasting Farm.

III

I spent the next year having many conversations with my little voice. Some days I felt as if I should be punished for what I had done in Belarus. I was angry at myself for having illusions about the Soviet way of life. I put my silver diary in a cupboard; I couldn't bear to throw it away, but I couldn't bear to read it again, either.

One night by the fire, surrounded by my wet and loving dogs, I had a sort of internal power surge, a glow that gave me a feeling of total bliss. A natural calm came over me at that moment, something I can't really explain. (Later, I'd discover that C.S. Lewis called this feeling "sudden joy.") With the calmness came a deep awareness of nature and of humanity.

After that I had this "sudden joy" experience from time to time. "I am no more important than an ant," I remember thinking once, "no more of a miracle than a violet." With that realization, I was filled with compassion for everything and everyone.

Somehow the experience of being locked up in Belarus made it possible for me to know another type of mind – I think it is what people might call the soul. It is what I call infinity.

It was on a morning amidst all these revelations that the desire to buy the Spooky Place overtook me. As fate would have it, I had come into some money that same week. The dogs and I turned off Glamorgan Road to walk up the driveway, full of potholes and littered with trash, towards the great, looming cross-shaped barn. The building was open to the outdoors, and a few streams of sunlight filtered through the boarded-up windows. I went up an old wooden ladder to the loft. Birds were nesting high in the red cedar rafters. As I sat there, I felt a curious energy go through me. It wasn't the "sudden joy" I'd been experiencing but a calm and good feeling coming from the barn loft itself. The barn seemed to speak to me, almost as if it were smiling.

By nightfall I had bought Glamorgan Farm. I hadn't even seen the house or the other structures. "Without so much as an inspection?" asked the shocked real estate woman. "It just feels right," I said. "I belong here."

Sometimes I still can't believe the barn is mine. I don't really feel as if I own it, in fact, because its historic, stoic grandness seems so much bigger than any one person. I feel that I am simply its keeper. It lends itself to many community and cultural events in the most elegant style, seating over two hundred local residents on its shiplap-decked floor. Tables of snacks and bottles of wine are laid out in one wing, and every so often a bird's nest will fall from the rafters onto the plates of hummus below. Paintings are hung on the walls, and microphones are set up for poetry readings and musical performances.

Before each event, in the lull before people begin parking on the road and ambling up the driveway, I sit in the loft alone and offer a thank you to the barn. It is like a little prayer I say – a barn prayer.

Barn Dance

IF THERE WAS EVER a space that lent itself to a country barn dance, it is the spacious log barn on Glamorgan Farm. One Thanksgiving, as a fundraiser for a group devoted to cleaning up our local streams, I decided to hold a traditional country dance with dinner. Publicity posters went out all over the community.

HELP SAVE OUR LOCAL SALMON STREAMS

COUNTRY BARN DANCE AT HISTORIC GLAMORGAN FARM

– LIVE MUSIC WITH CALLER –

GREAT THANKSGIVING GRUB, PIE-EATING CONTEST,

PRIZES AND MORE!

DRESS APPROPRIATELY

We swept the loft's wooden decking floor with long push brooms. The barn is so massive that the upper floor had to be designed in a curve, the centre being the highest point, to hold the weight. Since the barn is built in a cross-shaped design, we planned to have the food in one wing, the band in the opposite wing, and the entire length of the central part as the dance floor. We placed straw bales around the perimeter for people to sit on.

The barn is very sound, barely shifting in our frequent, small, rattling earthquakes. Only a bit of exterior rot can be seen on the ends of the logs, and birds and butterflies make interesting homes in the powdery material there. The cedar beams give off a real barn smell. In preparation for the dance, I had the roof power-washed, painted the heavy door light grey and had some glass replaced in the paned windows.

The night of the event was clear and mild, with a full moon. We had strung white lights in the poplars along the driveway, around the doorway to the barn and in the wild currant bushes. There were displays of pumpkins and squashes picked that day in the Healthy Harvest meadow. The oak-barrel tubs by the door and along the driveway were full of fading nasturtiums and begonias.

A committee of six women from the salmon stream society had cooked all day at home, and they brought the food over in a van. Warm plates of carved turkey, cranberry sauce, turnips,

THE GREAT BARN

Ink with watercolour by Bruno Bobak

salad and pumpkin pie were carried up the stairs and placed on
the red-checkered tablecloths just before people arrived. The
band arrived too, bearded, middle-aged men in plaid shirts and
corduroys carrying fiddles and banjos.

People began to stroll up the driveway as the sun sank
behind the distant hills. The women wore denim skirts and flowery blouses. The men wore jeans and bolo ties, silver belt buck-
les and Stetsons. I gave a brief farm tour to a small group who
arrived early, pointing out the iron door hinges forged in 1900,
the heirloom pumpkins planted by David in the front field, the
Naked Neck hens, which were going in to roost for the evening, and the woolly Russian horse, who hung his big head over
the fence because he didn't want to be left out. As we rounded the final corner, we could smell turkey wafting from the loft

and hear the fiddles. More people arrived, a few women carrying pies. Soon the bales of straw were covered with people balancing paper plates laden with slabs of turkey and pie. Some sat outside on the wooden slatted benches, enjoying mugs of cider as the autumn mist settled over the pasture.

After dinner the band began with a lively square dance, and several groups of squares formed. Partners were bowing to each other and grinning from ear to ear. Those who belonged to square-dance clubs were elegant and light on their feet; others had a great time mixing up their left and their right and needing to be pushed towards their next partner. The sashay in the Virginia Reel took up the length of the barn. During the breaks, there were games: apple bobbing, pumpkin bowling and squash-pip spitting. The winners received prizes of red kerchiefs, felt insoles, packages of seeds and cans of baked beans. The children had found all the old carts in the yard and were busy having sulky races in the meadow under the harvest moon.

In the middle of the second heat of the ladies' pie-eating contest, a group of children burst into the loft shouting, "The police are here! The fire truck is here!" My heart sank. What to do, what to do? Should I say I was having a private party? That would be legal, even if a fundraiser wasn't.

The fire chief, with his blue uniform and his clipboard, came up the stairs followed by a policewoman. The finalists in the pie-eating contest looked up in horror, their faces covered with blueberry pie and gobs of vanilla ice cream.

"Piece of pie for my favourite fire chief and policewoman?"
I asked desperately. "Coffee?"

The place went quiet. The band's drummer played a drum
roll.

"Do you have a fire exit?" the fire chief asked.

"Do you have a liquor licence?" asked the policewoman.

"Well," I began slowly, "there is an exit door on the end
of each wing." Everyone seemed relieved. "The problem is, I
haven't gotten around to building the steps to go with them. But
the doors work fine, and they're not that high off the ground."
There was no response, so I kept going. "Besides, these are all
my friends and we're just having a party."

The fire chief walked over and looked at each of the loft
doors, which swung open to reveal the moon above the trees.
The policewoman sat on a bale of straw, and somebody gave her
a mug of coffee. After a minute, the chief rejoined us and sat
down next to the policewoman on the straw.

"As for the liquor licence," I offered, "people donated the
cider, and it was free to everyone. You know, we took donations.
We are trying to raise money to clean up the salmon streams in
North Saanich."

"We have a winner!" called the judge of the pie-eating
contest. The winner was a woman with a yellow and turquoise
crinoline and blueberry pie all down the front of her dress.

"Excuse me," I said to the fire chief and the policewoman, "but I must award the prize."

I presented the woman in the stained crinoline with a huge Blue Hubbard squash picked earlier in the day. "And this prize was donated, ladies and gentlemen, by the disabled gardeners who garden in the front field of Glamorgan Farm," I announced loudly, so the fire chief and the policewoman could hear. Everyone clapped, and then the band began to play again and people got up to dance. They were doing another Virginia Reel.

The fire chief had his head in his hands. The policewoman stood up and adjusted her bulletproof vest.

"Would you like to dance?" I asked the chief.

"Oh, I suppose," he sighed in exasperation.

"I promise I'll get those stairs built by spring," I yelled to him as we did a twirl. He spun to his next partner, and they formed an arch for the rest of us to storm through.

The Biggest Death

WHAT IS REALLY FUN and relaxing on the farm is to have a friend over for dinner. I spend the day cleaning the house, ironing napkins, picking flowers, setting the table, and preparing a supper made from as many things raised and grown on the farm as possible. I get my chores finished and then make a jug of something to drink, full of ice and fruit, so that if it's nice weather my friend and I can sit on the sunny deck and catch up on our news while dinner cooks in the kitchen. Usually we'll take a walk around the farm before we eat, looking at the gardens and at the animals who are settling for the night – the ducks having their final wash of the day, the horses munching on their hay and the chickens slowly going in to roost. Often the gardeners in the community allotment plots are coiling up their hoses as David from the Healthy Harvest group closes up the greenhouse.

One evening I invited my good friend, Lorna, to supper.

We hadn't seen each other for ages – I had been so wrapped up in farm duties and Lorna, who is a poet, had been writing her latest book. Lorna arrived in a sad state. Her old cat, Dickens, had been run over earlier in the week. Being run over is such an unnatural way to die, and so undignified. The driver hadn't even stopped, and it was a neighbour who carried Dickens to Lorna's porch. So Lorna was grief-stricken, but I was hoping a good supper would help her mood.

I had prepared a duck for us, one that I had raised. I raise my ducks for a good eight months, and they have a joyous life in the outdoors with lots of pools to swim in and good grain to eat in the company of their brothers and sisters. I'd filled the roast duck with a stuffing I make from blackberries, other farm fruit and pumpkin, and made a big salad with Gavin's wild Glamorgan greens.

Lorna and I sipped my drink concoction from our tall glasses and then took a stroll along the gravel paths between the barns. One of the little roads is called Patrick Lane, after Lorna's partner, also a poet. I was boarding a few horses at the time, and they were standing still in the upper field, tails switching at the occasional fly. The turkeys were pecking at the last of their corn. The two large pigs, Mabel and Matilda, lying in their mud bed, let out a grunt or two as we passed. Lorna laughed. "It's like a medieval village here," she said.

By the time we got back, the kitchen smelled of duck and

the fresh bouquet of sweet peas I'd picked. A rhubarb pie was in the oven. We sat down and made a toast to Dickens, then to Kyle and Nappy and to Merlin – we were a little sentimental, but that was okay. I carved the duck, which was cooked perfectly and fell off the bone. As we ate, Lorna and I got talking about the two strange trips we'd taken together a few years earlier.

The first trip was to Malaysia. Lorna was there to read for the Commonwealth Games, and the organizers had put us up in a five-star hotel. What a hotel it was – the most luxurious hotel in Kuala Lumpur! We found the place to be such a paradox: the wealth and growth of a capitalist country and the strict law that would cane a person if he or she so much as dropped a gum wrapper on the pristine streets. There was absolutely no crime in the city. We walked at midnight through the downtown area, up back alleys and through wooded parks, passing two shimmering blue glass towers on our way – the highest in the world, the brochures said.

Our second trip was to a monkey-rescue farm in eastern Canada. The woman who runs it rescues chimpanzees from scientific laboratories in the United States. Lorna and I were going to volunteer there for a few days, and then I planned to continue on to Fredericton to visit Mum and Dad.

There were sixteen chimps in residence. They had been used for disease research, so most of them had AIDS or hepatitis. The place was full of ladders, ropes and platforms for the chimps to climb on. There were outdoor pens with swing sets and sand-boxes and even plastic toys for the chimps to play with. Our volunteer work consisted of preparing afternoon snacks for the chimps. Each chimp received a brown paper bag full of treats: three peppermints, two marshmallows, a red licorice stick, five cashews and a dried apricot. Lorna and I have laughed since then about the candy; I think that's easier for us to do than talk-ing about the pain and suffering humans have inflicted on chim-panzees.

After we'd finished reminiscing, I was explaining to Lorna how I made the duck stuffing when there was a frantic knock at the door. It was the owner of an Arabian horse I was boarding — a large woman in jodhpurs, red-faced and anxious. Between puffs of breath, she managed to explain, "It's the Sheik! I think he's broken his leg." The woman dialed the veterinarian's num-ber with shaking hands, and then we all went out to look at the horse.

The Sheik was standing in the field holding up a thin, quiv-ering leg. He clearly had a broken cannon bone. I ran cold water from the hose on his leg to ease his pain while the owner quiet-ly stroked his face. Soon the veterinarian arrived in his mobile equine hospital. He wore blue overalls and carried a black plas-tic tray full of bottles and implements. He took one look at the horse's leg and told the owner that the Sheik would have to be put down. I held the horse while the vet prepared two needles,

one to relax the horse, the other to stop the animal's heart. I
didn't mention calling Fred about the backhoe, but I knew that
would be my next task.

After the second injection, the horse fell to the ground and
let out a groan. There was a precise second – and it happens with
every death on the farm, natural or otherwise – where the animal is still physically alive but no longer has a sense of where or
what it is. That's the moment that's so difficult for *us*, but for the
animals I am always relieved, almost envious sometimes.

I slipped off the Sheik's halter and handed it to his sad owner at the fence. The vet did one final check with his stethoscope
as he knelt in the damp evening grass. "He's gone," the vet said,
and by that time so was the sun. It was a chilly night, and I could
see that Lorna was cold.

"Let's cover him up with blankets for the night," I suggested
to the owner. "I'll call Fred in the morning, and then you can
make a beautiful grave."

Lorna and I returned to my warm kitchen. I stoked the fire
and gave her a sweater, and we sat down to finish our duck.

About a month later, our local palliative care facility held
a poetry reading as a fundraiser. Lorna read a poem called "At
Anny's Stable," and the first words were "The biggest death I'd
ever seen."

At Anny's Stable

The biggest death
I'd ever seen, anything
that was light,
that was wind,
gone out of him.

The vet who put him down
knelt by his side,
removed his shoes,
one leg resting on the other,
back and front,
and gave them to the woman
who was weeping.

Next morning
before the backhoe
I go out again.

He's on his back,
legs straight up and stiff,
his mouth twists into a grin –
more happiness than anyone wants to know.

Maybe this is where
the legends begin – Pegasus
and Horses of the Sun.

His hooves, unnailed,
run on clouds and sky,
and the flies
bridling his chestnut head
are really
the noisiest of angels

flown so far
you can see right through
their wings.

—Lorna Crozier

Blackberry Duck Stuffing

This stuffing is made entirely from fruit and vegetables. Blackberries are the main ingredient and offer the most flavour. You can pick them from the hedgerows in August, and they freeze very well, too. They are delicious cooked with duck.

Mix a cup of blackberries with a cup of squash or pumpkin purée. (I often use purée from an heirloom French Rouge pumpkin grown on the farm.) Add a cup of other fruit – cut-up apples, pears and peaches work well. Add some fresh herbs, such as rosemary, thyme and oregano, to taste. In the autumn, if you know your mushrooms, you can pick field mushrooms and add some spongy boletus to the stuffing. The boletus has a thick, rich texture and makes a lovely complement to the fruit. Stuff the duck, then cook it slowly, preferably in a clay pot. Keep the bird wet by pouring leftover stuffing over it and adding fruit juice as needed.

I serve this duck with baked yams and a salad of wild greens from the farm.

Dinty Moore Comes to Tea

LAST SPRING MUM came to visit for a week. I rarely plan anything on the first day she is here, because I know she wants to
rest after her long airplane journey. We putter around the farm,
perhaps making a small bonfire to burn the limbs that have fallen
in the last windstorm, or picking nettles and making soup.

Mum had had a long icy winter, endless sleeting days of fro-
zen sidewalks that kept her confined to the house. "And Bruno
has that damned CNN on all day!" she moaned during one of
our telephone calls. "Thank God for that book you sent me at
Christmas, Thackeray's *Book of Snobs*. It's so funny, even though
I can only read two pages at a time with my failing eyes." For
months we had had lengthy phone conversations about how winter drags on. "At least you can get out and walk the dogs," she'd
say. "All the postmen here have broken arms!"

On the second day of her visit, we went to Sidney to do a

few errands. Mum always gets her hair trimmed by Olga at the same place that does my hair. Mum says, after they hug, "Oh, Olga, just tidy it up," which only takes twenty minutes. She doesn't want a shampoo, not even a blow-dry, so Olga simply wets Mum's white-haired head and cuts off a few thin hairs. Still, Mum says it's the best haircut she has ever had.

I love Olga too, although I pay her a fortune for colour, highlights and styling. I get pedicures there as well, by Sheena, because I have thick calluses on the soles of my feet from wearing rubber boots all day. (Imagine getting a pedicure when I spend most of my afternoons shovelling manure. *I* should be in *The Book of Snobs*. In the summer I also get my toenails painted, because maybe I'll wear sandals one day, and you never know who might notice. But actually one does not wear sandals on a farm unless one wants to get one's toes crushed under a limb or a hoof or a mower.) My pedicure is the one time I allow myself to read *People* and *Hello* magazines. I sit on a big vinyl chair on a spotless white towel, my feet soaking in warm water and bubbles, and for one hour I can look all I want at glossy photographs of dowdy Camilla Parker-Bowles in a mauve satin gown at some charity fundraiser, Prince William with his new girlfriend or George Bush's daughter being arrested for drunk driving. When the pedicure is over, I always have a split second of regret that I have to go outside, back to the world of living and coping.

Sidney is a seaside town very close to rural North Saanich.

It is where we go to do our errands, the other side of the highway. The powers that be have tried to make the town quaint by putting cobblestone sidewalks, benches, flower boxes and banners along the main street and preserving the heritage post office, but really Sidney is a chamber-of-commerce kind of town. Starbucks, McDonald's and tacky dollar stores keep popping up. There are a few trendy shops: the House Dressing Company, where you can buy bendy-stemmed, bead-encrusted martini glasses for twenty dollars each, and an olde English sweet shoppe, full of colourful candies in glass jars and imported teas and biscuits. By far the most charming aspect of Sidney is that it is a "book town." There are bookstores all down Beacon Avenue and off on the side streets. One sells only books on military topics, another on boating, another on gardening. The Haunted Bookshop sells rare and used books and next door is another shop which sells old books and antiques; its window displays worn leather books, glass lanterns, ivory-handled writing utensils and ink pots. Clive Tanner, who is promoting Sidney as a "book town," told me that such a place in England boasts a tiny store that sells only books on bees and honey. I go to Tanners to buy the *The Globe and Mail* or to pick up ferry schedules and free local magazines, which are increasingly full of advertisements for yoga lessons and spa treatments featuring hot rocks.

While Mum is having her hair cut, I usually go to the post office, buy birdseed from the pet store for my finches and return my library books. Mum is always ready with her coat on when I get back to Olga's, and then we go on to a couple of thrift stores. Mum likes to buy cheap used jeans and white shirts, and we are always on the lookout for flannelette nightshirts for Dad.

We start at the PCS thrift shop. It has a musty smell that reminds me of summers spent with my Polish grandparents in Toronto, in their grey-green, asphalt-shingled house on Ossington Avenue. The smell was a combination of old carpet and steaming potatoes and cabbage.

That day, like every other, Mum sifted through the racks of used clothing, surrounded by swag lamps, cheap brass candlesticks, ceramic candy dishes, chipped Arborite coffee tables and plastic flowers. She found a pair of Calvin Klein jeans for herself for three dollars. I found a pink polyester nightshirt for Dad, a joke. It cost two dollars. It had a dumb yellow plastic decal of a chicken on it that read, "I got laid in Alaska." Mum and I were in gales of laughter as we bought it.

Next we decided to visit the dollar store. We looked at the iron candle holders, bulk packages of dried noodles and pink scented soaps. The plastic dolls, the rubber spiders, the scrub brushes and spatulas were all a dollar, but everything I liked was at least $3.50. We bought six pale-blue Chinese cereal bowls, very plain and simple. Mum was hesitant at first. "They are lovely, but think of the poor woman turning them out all day in a hot factory for pennies." It was true, but I really loved those bowls.

I wanted flax muffins at the local coffee shop, the kind of establishment that sells low-fat, decaf, double-shot, three-layer organic soy lattes, with or without cinnamon. We bought the muffins and then headed for the liquor store in the Safeway mall, our final stop. The Sidney liquor store is a specialty shop. There is a French vodka called Grey Goose for fifty dollars, a brand of Russian vanilla vodka and an Italian organic wine. Mum wanted Scotch: "The cheap stuff," she said.

Once our shopping was finished, we crossed the congested, freshly paved parking lot. Sidney is always paving, and the two-way stops keep being changed to four-way stops. It is common to see a confused senior, either on a motorized scooter or in a lumbering cream-coloured Oldsmobile, stopped in the middle of an intersection, with everybody else honking.

Suddenly, without warning, Mum was lying on the pavement. One second I was looking at our car several yards away, with the two hairy dogs in the back, noses pressed to the glass, and the next moment Mum had fallen. Her head was up against the back tire of another car.

Before I managed to say anything, she was sitting up, but she seemed stunned. She had on a thin white shirt, and I could see that she had a small but deep gash on her right arm. She was still holding the Scotch. I said to Mum, "Good job, Old Pup — you still have the bottle intact!"

"Old Pup" is Mum's nickname. I have a friend who introduced us to this funny "road sister" gimmick. The Road Sisters are a feminist rebel group of women who like to go on road trips together. Every road sister has an alias, formed by combining the name of the first pet you owned with the name of the first street you lived on. My road sister name is Gracie Grey, and Mum's is Old Pup Raeside. So I said, "Good job, Old Pup" about the bottle, and helped her to her feet.

We stood there for a moment. Aside from the gash on her arm, Mum seemed to be okay. Once we got into the car and shut the doors, we both relaxed. Mum said, "It's so humiliating to fall," and I said, "Let's go home and you can lie on the sofa. I'll make tea and put on Elgar."

"Oh, I love Elgar," Old Pup said.

When we got back to the farm, I put Mum on the couch in the living room and covered her with a woollen blanket she had sent me one Christmas. It was handwoven by an old Acadian woman, and the pattern was supposed to resemble a loon. Soft green light, filtered through the honeysuckle, plum trees and tall pines surrounding the house, came through the panes of wavy glass. I put on Elgar's *Enigma Variations*, which always makes me very emotional. The dogs gathered around the base of the sofa. Dogs always know when you have been rattled.

Mum drifted off to sleep under the loon blanket, and I went to my office to make lists, pay bills and calm down. As I was paying my pest-control bill, the phone rang. It was a nice-sounding woman who said she had heard that my mother was in town. Her dad, Dinty Moore, had been in the same kindergarten class as Mum (this was seventy-eight years ago), and Dinty would love to meet up with Mum, if only for a short while. Could we manage something? I wrote down her number and told her I would call her back.

I took the message in to Mum, who was now awake. "You have a call from Dinty Moore," I said. "Do you know him?"

Mum gazed at the ceiling for a minute, then burst out laughing. "Yes," she said. "It was at Burnaby Lake, in kindergarten. There were lily pads on the lake, and we were in Miss Harry's class. Miss Harry wore irons – leg braces – and Barbara and I were sitting at a little wooden table when a boy named Dinty Moore came into the room. He was younger than we were, so he joined the class late. He was crying, I remember. Miss Harry dragged herself across the room and sat him down, and then she put a Christmas cracker decal on his knee. Barbara and I were *so* jealous!"

We agreed that I would call Dinty's daughter and invite them out to the farm. Mum is very social. She's the type who likes it when people drop in, whereas I run upstairs if I hear a knock on the door, and spy through the curtains. A date was set for coffee the following evening.

The next day was difficult, because Mum's arm really hurt. We sat outside in the sun, and I washed it with salt water. Mum

was obsessed with looking at her wound, and we finally decided to go to the walk-in clinic. Mum wore her new thrift shop
Calvin Klein jeans. The doctor gave her four stitches, and then
Mum and I went for a walk on the beach. Sidney has a lovely
pebble beach with clear salt water, and most of the time seals
are bobbing close to shore. When we got back, we had a bonfire
in the field. After supper, Mum lay on the sofa, and I began the
preparations to receive Dinty. I made coffee and set out some
gingersnaps and my enamelled mugs from Chinatown. Once
everything was ready, I joined Mum in the living room to wait.

There was a knock at the door. I jumped up and opened it,
and there they were – Dinty, tall and charming, dressed in off-
white and khaki, with grey hair and wearing a big grin. His wife
stood beside him in a red dress and flowery coat. His daughter,
who had her father's smile, was wearing a lime-green pantsuit.

"Come in, come in," I welcomed them. "Mum is dying to see
you." Mum got up as I led them into the living room and gave
Dinty a hug. They fell to chatting right away. The visitors didn't
want coffee, they said. They could only stay for a short time.

Dinty looked really good for his age. (Remember, he was six
months younger than Mum.) He had never had a fall, he told us.
"It's my eyes," Mum said. "It's not the actual fall so much as the
fact of being mortified."

"And at Safeway," I added, wishing we could change the
subject.

Dinty and his wife described their life in Victoria. They went to potlucks and walked among the rhododendrons along the seawall wearing matching fleece vests. Their daughter lived nearby.

When Dinty and his family left, I said to Mum, "They are really lucky – they're so happy." And then I ate all the gingersnaps.

After Mum and I did our nightly ablutions, we finished off the evening with *Peter the Great,* the chapter describing how Peter's followers were thrown from balconies and impaled on the iron gates surrounding the Kremlin, and how young Peter watched from the balcony, hiding in terror behind a red velvet curtain.

We put Ozonol on Mum's wound and changed the bandage before going to bed.

Mum said from across the dark hall, "Dinty Moore. I can't believe it."

"Yes, I'm glad we met him," I replied. "Good night, Old Pup."

Nettle Soup

Nettles are very high in iron. On Glamorgan Farm they grow like a forest around the septic field and in the horse paddock. Pick only the tender tops in early spring. Wear rubber gloves, because nettles sting.

Fill a saucepan with nettle tops. Boil with a little water, salt and pepper, a cut-up onion and 2 minced cloves of garlic. Once the tops have boiled down, pour the mixture into the blender, along with some cream or milk or yogourt – the amount depends on how creamy you like your soup. Blend until the mixture is smooth and the nettle tops have dissolved into the liquid.

Pour the mixture back into a saucepan. Simmer on low, adding grated cheese to taste. Goat cheese also gives this soup a great flavour.

Serve with plain yogourt and a huge basket of fresh bread.

Variation: Boil the nettle tops with very little water and then drain. Stir into scrambled eggs or fold into an omelette. Top with goat cheese.

YOUNG ANNY SLEEPING

Charcoal drawing by Bruno Bobak

Evening

THE CHORES ON Glamorgan Farm in the early evening include feeding all the animals and making sure that they are secure from predators and bad weather for the night. The pigs are given a banana or apple snack up in their barn, where they sleep in contentment in a deep bed of straw. The ducks are given some bread before being locked in their tin shack with a clean tub of water, just in case they get up in the night and want to have a bath. The chickens have a condominium situation, permitting them to roost in order of power, seniority and self-esteem. The Naked Necks claim the top tier, and there is one Barred Rock rooster with a club foot who always gets relegated to the floor. The horses usually go out to the large meadow, where they can stand under the Garry oak trees if it rains. However, if it is terribly stormy, wet or cold, the horses stay indoors, where they are covered with thick blankets and get to eat hot bran mash with molasses. A final stroll around the barns, checking for lights left on, open windows or suspicious-looking characters, completes my routine.

Often, in my nightie and rubber boots, I'll sit in my garden and watch the dusk fall under a golden sky. As I look around, I can hardly believe the place is mine. Sometimes I feel as if I am surrounded by farm cathedrals.

When the darkness is complete and the air has become damp, I go into the house to make myself a martini with a big slice of lemon, on ice. While it sits, I light a fire. In front of the fireplace I have a big, comfy chair, a stack of books and a notebook. In the notebook I make lists of things to do and things I need. At the top of my list this week is buying a foot bath – the type you plug in so the water can massage your tired, hot feet.

At bedtime I have a bath upstairs in the tiny bathroom. When I first moved into the house, I managed to find a small tub, the old-fashioned kind with claw feet. When I sit in the tub, I can look out the window, over the rolling meadow where the horses are resting. A jar of dark pink tulips sits on the old metal washstand. I lie in the bath and know contentment.

Then I go to bed, under the faded blue eiderdown that belonged to my grandfather. In winter, I take a hot water bottle with me. And I am always joined by Baby Alice Mary,

Havel and Kitty. When the weather is warm, I leave the window wide open so that I can listen to the choir of frogs in the nearby pond, singing their mighty evening song.

And then I get a damn leg cramp.

Acknowledgements

Many people contributed to the making of this book. My thanks go to my parents, Bruno Bobak and Molly Lamb Bobak for their wonderful illustrations; to Lorna Crozier, Susan Musgrave and P.K. Page for the inclusion of their special poems; to Robbyn Gordon and Greg Aspa for their evocative photographs; to Frances Hunter for the beautiful design; to Neil and Jean Reimer for telling me much about North Saanich history. Clive and Christine Tanner, Marilyn Mortimer-Lamb, Ann Saddlemyer and Joan Coldwell helped in ways too numerous to mention and I am grateful to them all. Finally, many thanks to my editor Barbara Pulling, who drew the whole thing together.

An earlier version of "Pickled Eggs" appeared in *Reading the Peninsula: Stories of the Saanich Peninsula*, edited by Sara Dowse (Community Arts Council of the Saanich Peninsula: 2003).

The poem "At Anny's Stable" will appear in slightly different form in Lorna Crozier's forthcoming collection *Whetstone*, to be published by McClelland and Stewart Ltd. in 2005.

About the illustrators

Molly Lamb Bobak was born in Burnaby, British Columbia, in 1920. She studied art under Jack Shadbolt at the Vancouver School of Art and joined the Canadian army in 1942, becoming the only female uniformed war artist in 1945. After the war, Molly married fellow Canadian war artist Bruno Bobak, and they had two children.

Now settled in Fredericton, New Brunswick, Molly continues to make regular visits to the West Coast. Although her sight is failing, she still paints small watercolours of North Saanich wildflowers and scenes from Pacific Rim National Park.

Bruno Bobak was born in Wawelowka, Poland, in 1923. He trained as an artist in Toronto, Ontario, and went on to become one of Canada's youngest war artists, commissioned in 1944. After the war ended, Bruno and his wife, Molly Lamb Bobak, painted and exhibited throughout Europe. In 1960, they moved to Fredericton, New Brunswick, where Bruno was appointed artist in residence at the university. From 1962 until his retirement in 1987, Bruno was director of the University of New Brunswick Art Centre.

Bruno spends his retirement gardening (he recently grafted a tomato, naming it "Bruno's Best") and fishing on the Saint John and Miramichi rivers.

ILLUSTRATIONS

About the Author

Anny Scoones was born in 1957. She was raised in Fredericton, New Brunswick, but spent summers with her grandmother on Galiano Island, British Columbia. After travelling abroad and in Canada as part of a theatre production crew, she settled on Galiano before moving to her present home in North Saanich.

An elected councillor for the District of North Saanich, Anny's special concerns are the protection of the environment, the preservation of heritage, the development of parks and bicycle paths, architectural planning and design, and support of agriculture in this rural area.

Anny has owned historic Glamorgan Farm since 2000. She is committed to restoring the farm's heritage buildings, raising rare breeds of livestock and growing heirloom produce. Her writings on these subjects have appeared in magazines and story collections. With a B.Ed. from the University of Victoria and a Diploma of Humanities, Anny is now working towards a Diploma in Cultural Restoration, which will augment her work both in the public sphere and on Glamorgan Farm.

Author photograph by Greg Aspa